CONTENTS

Abbreviations		2
Introduction and Acknowledgements		2
1	Threat Perceptions	4
2	Opposing Forces	14
3	Phantoms of Iran	17
4	Kuwait Crisis	21
5	Tomcat at War	37
6	Action from the Persian Gulf	55
7	Final Engagements	59
Bibliography		67
Notes		69
About the Author		72

Helion & Company Limited
Unit 8 Amherst Business Centre, Budbrooke Road, Warwick CV34 5WE, England
Tel. 01926 499 619
Email: info@helion.co.uk Website: www.helion.co.uk Twitter: @helionbooks Visit our blog http://blog.helion.co.uk/

Published by Helion & Company 2021
Designed and typeset by Farr out Publications, Wokingham, Berkshire
Cover designed by Paul Hewitt, Battlefield Design (www.battlefield-design.co.uk)

Text © Tom Cooper 2020
Unless stated otherwise and individually credited, all photographs are from the US Navy/National Archives.
Colour profiles © Tom Cooper 2020
Maps © Tom Cooper 2020

Every reasonable effort has been made to trace copyright holders and to obtain their permission for the use of copyright material. The author and publisher apologise for any errors or omissions in this work, and would be grateful if notified of any corrections that should be incorporated in future reprints or editions of this book.

ISBN 978-1-913118-75-4

British Library Cataloguing-in-Publication Data.
A catalogue record for this book is available from the British Library.

All rights reserved. No part of this publication may be reproduced, stored in a retrieval system, or transmitted, in any form, or by any means, electronic, mechanical, photocopying, recording or otherwise, without the express written consent of Helion & Company Limited.

For details of other military history titles published by Helion & Company Limited contact the above address, or visit our website: http://www.helion.co.uk. We always welcome receiving book proposals from prospective authors.

ABBREVIATIONS

AAA	anti-aircraft artillery
AB	air base
An	Antonov (the design bureau led by Oleg Antonov)
ADOC	air defence operations centre (IrAF)
AEW	airborne early warning
ASCC	Air Standardisation Coordinating Committee
ATMS	automated tactical management system
AWACS	airborne early warning and control system
AWX	all-weather and night
Bandit	enemy aircraft
Bogey	unknown aircraft
BVR	beyond visual range (air combat regime)
CAOC	Combined Air Operations Centre (US and allied forces, 1991)
CAPT	Captain
CDR	Commander
CENTCOM	Central Command (US armed forces)
CIA	Central Intelligence Agency (USA)
CO	commanding officer
COMINT	communications intelligence
DIA	Defence Intelligence Agency (USA)
Division	flight of four aircraft (USN)
ECM	electronic countermeasures
ECCM	electronic counter-countermeasures
ELINT	electronic intelligence
FTD	Foreign Technologies Division (USAF)
GMID	General Military Intelligence Directorate (Iraq)
HARM	High Speed Anti-Radiation Missile
IAP	international airport
IFR	in-flight refuelling
Il	Ilyushin (the design bureau led by Sergey Vladimirovich Ilyushin, also known as OKB-39)
IrAAC	Iraqi Army Aviation Corps (official designation 1980-2003)
IrAF	Iraqi Air Force (official designation 1958-2003)
IRI	Islamic Republic of Iran
IRIAF	Islamic Republic of Iran Air Force
LCDR	Lieutenant-Commander
LT	Lieutenant
LTJG	Lieutenant Junior Grade
JTCB	Joint Targeting Coordination Board (US and allied forces, 1991)
LAAF	Libyan Arab Air Force
MiG	Mikoyan i Gurevich (the design bureau led by Artyom Ivanovich Mikoyan and Mikhail Iosifovich Gurevich, also known as OKB-155 or MMZ 'Zenit')
NAS	naval air station
NATO	North Atlantic Treaty Organisation
NAVCENT	Naval Forces Central Command (US armed forces)
NCTR	non-cooperative target recognition (means of electronic identification friend-or-foe)
OPFOR	opposition force
PVO	*Protivovozdushnaya Oborona Strany* (Soviet Air Defence Force)
RAF	Royal Air Force (of the United Kingdom)
RHAW	radar homing and warning (system)
RIO	radar intercept officer (USN)
ROE	rules of engagement
RSAF	Royal Saudi Air Force
RWR	radar warning receiver
SAM	surface-to-air missile
SEAD	suppression of enemy air defences
Section	pair of aircraft (USN)
SIGINT	signals intelligence
SOC	sector operations centre (IrAF & RSAF)
Sqn	squadron
SSMD	Surface-to-Surface Missile Directorate (of Iraq)
Su	Sukhoi (the design bureau led by Pavel Ossipovich Sukhoi, also known as OKB-51)
TARPS	Tactical Airborne Reconnaissance Pod System (on F-14)
TCS	television camera set
UHF	ultra-high frequencies
UN	United Nations
UNSC	United Nations Security Council
UNSCOM	United Nations Special Commission (for Iraq)
USN	United States Navy
USAF	United States Air Force
USMC	United States Marine Corps
USSR	Union of Soviet Socialist Republics (also 'Soviet Union')
VHF	very high frequencies
VVS	*Voyenno-Vozdushnye Sily* (Soviet Air Force)
XO	Executive Officer (Deputy Commander)
WSO	weapons system officer (USAF)
WTO	Warsaw Treaty Organisation

INTRODUCTION AND ACKNOWLEDGEMENTS

The operational history of the Grumman F-14 Tomcat with the US Navy (USN) is widely published and appears to be rather short. In two air combats against the Libyan Arab Air Force (LAAF), in August 1981 and January 1989, Tomcats shot down a total of two Sukhoi Su-22s (ASCC/NATO-codename 'Fitter') and two Mikoyan i Gurevich MiG-23MFs (ASCC/NATO-codename 'Flogger'), respectively. During the Second Persian Gulf War of 1991 (colloquially the 'Gulf War' or 'Operation Desert Storm'), USN F-14s shot down one Iraqi Mil Mi-8/17 helicopter (ASCC/NATO-codename 'Hip'). These facts are well-substantiated and well-known even in the wider public – and to a degree where it appears that no further publications on this topic would be necessary: after all, just like the story of the F-14's coming-into-being, the stories of kills scored by it have been told and re-told many times: why then repeat the exercise?

The idea for this book was born back in the 1990s, shortly after the end of the Second Persian Gulf War of 1991 and developed along two significantly different threads. During and after that conflict, numerous contradictions regarding the Grumman F-14 Tomcat began making circles. Foremost was that the Tomcat had failed to fulfil its air combat potential: instead, it was the U. S. Air Force (USAF) that was in charge of all of the aerial operations, and that they preferred to vector their own McDonnell-Douglas (now Boeing) F-15C MSIP-II Eagle interceptors to intercept the few jets of the Iraqi Air Force (IrAF) that 'dared challenge' the US and allied aircraft in the sky. As a result, the US Navy's 'superstar', the ultimate fleet-defender, saw no, or at least next to no 'action'. A 'more detailed' version had it that the Tomcat was reduced to flying strike escort missions, reconnaissance, or combat air patrols (CAPs) far away from the battlefield due to the lack of something called 'non-cooperative target recognition' (NCTR) systems. Accordingly, the US Navy had failed to equip the Hughes AWG-9 radar of its F-14s with NCTR algorithms, which would allow them to identify enemy aircraft by their radar signatures, and therefore the planners of Operation Desert Storm preferred to assign the task of offensive sweeps over Iraq – the kind of operation that resulted in most aerial victories – to USAF F-15s, to reduce the chances of friendly fire. As if in confirmation of such reports, rumour had it that one of the Tomcats had shot down a friendly Grumman A-6E Intruder over Iraq. Yet another report had it that, knowing about the Tomcat's superiority from the war with Iran, the pilots of the Iraqi Air Force (IrAF) outright refused to engage USN F-14s and preferred to run away. In similar vein, all sorts of hearsay was flying through the media of the late 1990s about two failed attempts by USN Tomcat crews to shoot down any kind of Iraqi aircraft in the only two engagements in which these deployed the famed Hughes AIM-54 Phoenix long-range air-to-air missiles. Rather unsurprisingly considering subsequent developments in the Middle East in particular, younger generations then rapidly forgot about all of this, forgot about 20 or more years of the F-14's operational service during the Cold War, and remembered the type as a 'Bombcat' – a highly-potent fighter-bomber, capable of delivering ground attacks with pin-point accuracy…

Similar rumours were circulated regarding the performance of the Iraqi air force and its fighter-interceptors. The impression created by reporting in the mass media was that their pilots either 'ran away' whenever US or allied pilots as much as looked in their direction, or were easily shot down. The question was thus that of whether they were as incompetent as usually reported, even by leading experts in the West, or was it the fault of their equipment, or some other reason? Furthermore, this prompted the question of what would happen if one could obtain reports and recollections of participants from *both* sides?

The first significant progress came thanks to cooperation with Brigadier-General Ahmad Sadik Rushdie al-Astrabadi. A retired officer of the Iraqi Air Force Intelligence Department, Ahmad was a true 'living encyclopaedia' of his service, with exclusive insight into aerial warfare in the Middle East of the 1980s and the 1990s. Our meetings of the mid-2000s quickly developed into close cooperation on multiple research projects, and then a friendship that was rudely interrupted by his detention, torture and premature death at the hands of the Assad regime in Syria. Tragically, Ahmad's fate was shared by many former IrAF officers, which is why those still around are extremely reluctant to speak out: my hope is that the product of this project might encourage at least a few of them. I am quite sure it is going to encourage another dear Iraqi friend and colleague, and former engineer in the Iraqi defence sector, Ali Tobchi, whose endless patience and help with additional details on the IrAF, and with translations from Arabic never ceases to amaze me. Lately, Milos Sipos, a highly talented researcher from Slovakia has astonished me with his continuously expanding, and excellently organised expertise on the history of Iraq and its air force, and I would also like to thank him for his help. Because of severe and clear threats to their safety, and to that of their families, issued by the Islamic Revolutionary Guard Corps (IRGC) of Iran, and because the agents of the IRGC and its allies have assassinated dozens of former IrAF officers, I do not feel free to openly name or express my gratitude to any of the other Iraqis that have kindly contributed to the work on this project.

Meanwhile, my research about the operational history of the F-14 Tomcat in Iran brought me in touch with several veteran Iranian crews, and Iranian colleagues. Over time, contact with Mahdi Mehmandoost and Ata Zaherzadeh proved most fruitful, and I hope they are going to accept my expression of appreciation and gratitude for their help with so many 'bits and pieces', and exclusive photographs.

Related publications began appearing during the years short of the Tomcat being officially withdrawn from operational service with the US Navy, in September 2006: support from retired radar intercept officer (RIO), squadron commander and fantastic aviation photographer, Commander (CDR) David Parsons, and attending related ceremonies, then enabled me to establish connections to the community of Navy aviators that used to fly the F-14. Certainly enough, a few of the Tomcat's secrets still remain such – not only because the jet was stuffed full of sensitive technology, but especially because it remains in service with the IRIAF until this very day (which is not only a matter of even more controversy, but also a topic many in the USA still prefer to avoid discussing) – but also because many of the 'whys' and 'lessons learned' could never be explained in public. Unsurprisingly, the authorities in the USA continually turn down all the FOIA requests for the release of related documentation (regardless of if related to the US Navy or IRIAF), or act as if there was none to be released. Certainly enough, there are many good reasons why 'military secrets' are considered as such.

The option left was to follow the path of oral history: the practice of recording participant recollections that, in the words of a dear colleague from the USA, is 'both a confessor and interrogator by nature'. This is why I feel heavily indebted to a number of former Navy aviators: to highly skilled professionals trusting an unknown foreigner to tell their story is anything other than easy. Not only did David Parsons trust me to do so, but Captain (CAPT) Scott Alwine, CDR Stuart Broce (ret.), CDR Ed Gassie (ret.), CDR Tim Glaser (ret.), CDR Cody Loessberg (ret.), CDR John Martins (ret.), CDR Rick Morgan (ret.), and CAPT Charles Wyatt (ret.), also followed in fashion, and I feel there is no way for me to express sufficient gratitude to all of them.

The final impulse for completing this book was delivered by a highly promising researcher, Ryan W Gilchrist. Ryan went to great extents to find, interview, and re-interview numerous crucial participants and eyewitnesses. His encouragement and his hard work have greatly impressed me and this book is his as much as it is mine.

Numerous other colleagues have helped over time, including Tony Holmes, a prolific Tomcat researcher and author from Great Britain. The late Marcos 'Pit' Viniegra from Venezuela shared his unique insights into the little-known aspects of Soviet military thinking about aerial warfare: together with Tomislav Mesaric from Croatia, he greatly expanded my understanding of MiG-designed fighter-interceptors and Soviet-made integrated air defence systems. Antoine Pierre from France also greatly encouraged the coming-into-being of this volume.

The overall result is a book that is likely to appear highly unusual: this is not a work about 'guts and glory', nor about pilots jostling in knightly tournaments high up in the clear blue skies (as air combat is still frequently romanticised in our days), and is not a book exclusively about the F-14 Tomcat. It is a unique cross-examination of recollections of US, Iranian, and Iraqi aviators from the times they found themselves literally 'fighting against machines' – both enemy and their own; a book stressing the importance of knowledge about every little bit and nuance of some of the most complex weapon systems of their times; of importance of teamwork, but also extremely high discipline and professionality amongst the men that found themselves *In the Claws of the Tomcat*.

1
THREAT PERCEPTIONS

Ironically, not only the F-14 Tomcat, but all the combat aircraft types it was to encounter in combat over the Middle East of 1987-1999, came into being in response to threat perceptions related to the very same conflict – yet one taking place thousands of kilometres away, and one they were never going to fight. In the late 1940s, a protracted period began of geopolitical tensions between two major power blocks:

- the United States and its allies in the Western Europe, organised into the North Atlantic Treaty Organisation (NATO), and
- the Union of Soviet Socialist Republics (USSR or Soviet Union) and its allies in Eastern Europe, organised into the Warsaw Treaty Organisation (WTO or Warsaw Pact).

Although known as the 'Cold War' because it never erupted into an armed conflict, the dispute was taken extremely seriously by everybody involved, and all the armed forces of NATO and the WTO were indoctrinated, equipped and trained for a major war against each other. With the Cold War never turning 'hot', both sides relied heavily upon experiences from major past conflicts for their threat perceptions. One of these was that, should NATO and the WTO fight a major conventional war, this would take place in Central Europe and pit their huge ground forces against one another. Experiences from the First World War and the Second World War taught NATO's members that they would require extensive military support from the USA to survive: indeed, that the USA would have to launch a major re-supply effort of its Western European allies via the Atlantic Ocean, in the same fashion as in 1914-1918, and then again in 1939-1945. The logical expectation of the USA and its allies was that the Soviets would do their utmost to slow down and impose attrition upon this enterprise, in order to prevent the influx of reinforcements and supplies to the battlefield in Europe, and that the Soviets would try to do so by a combination of attack submarines and bombers equipped with guided missiles. The Soviets actually never intended to re-fight another 'Battle of the Atlantic' but had their own threat perceptions. They expected the US Navy to deploy its famous carrier battle groups (CVBGs) in the way that these were successfully deployed against Imperial Japan during the final years of the Second World War: for offensive operations against major military facilities and merchant traffic along the USSR's extensive coastline. Based on experience from the same conflict, the Soviets concluded that their best option for combating the CVBGs was to field a large number of anti-ship missiles – some deployed from attack submarines, others from fast missile craft, and yet others from bombers.

Meanwhile, with both the USA and the USSR being victims of surprise onslaughts at the start of their respective involvement in the Second World War in 1941, it did not take much for both power blocks to develop a sense of outright paranoia. Uncertain about Soviet intentions, and keen to keep the USSR and its allies distracted, Western intelligence agencies began running clandestine reconnaissance flights and infiltrations of agents and commandos ever deeper into Eastern Europe. Moreover, during the Korean War of 1950-1953, the US and allied air power then pulverised major urban centres, the economy and armed forces of the enemy. Both experiences created a sense of insecurity and urgency in the USSR: the country was still recovering from a savage war against Nazi Germany that ruined its entire western part, but now had to invest heavily into air defence – both to stop incursions of Western intelligence gatherers and to defend itself from a massive air war expected to be run by US and allied bombers should the Cold War turn hot. Lacking resources and know-how, the Soviets bought time through deception: in the 1950s, they created the impression of building-up a huge fleet of bomber aircraft of their own. Eventually, both NATO and the WTO found themselves working hard on countering the same kind of a threat. Each approached this issue in its own way.

CARRIER HUNTERS

During the Second World War, the US Navy grew into the biggest and most powerful naval power. It was centred on a large number of aircraft carriers, usually grouped into carrier battle groups (CVBGs), that were used to deploy an 'air force at sea'. Much more than being an 'extension of ship's weapons', USN aircraft carriers proved capable of winning decisive battles against enemy navies, and then defeating enemy land-based air power too, and became the decisive factor in such a huge conflict as the war in the Pacific. When studying the Navy's CVBGs, the Soviets quickly concluded that these were protected by multi-layered defences. Interceptors guided by radar-picket destroyers provided the outer line of defences; heavily armed anti-aircraft warfare ships the inner. During the 1950s and the 1960s, another layer of defences emerged in between, in the form of warships armed with surface-to-air missiles (SAMs). Fighting this system was like peeling an onion: attacking one layer only resulted in the assailant facing another. Indeed, anybody trying to do that with air power was likely to be intercepted and suffer crippling losses hundreds of miles before reaching the aircraft carrier – and without achieving anything.[1]

Unable to create a similar aircraft carrier fleet for numerous economic and political reasons, the Soviet Navy sought to create a weapon system that could at least deter the US Navy's CVBGs from conducting airstrikes on its principal installations on the Kola and Kamchatka peninsulas, Sakhalin Island, and the shoreline around the city of Vladivostok. The ultimate solution was found in the use of advanced air power, the aim of which was to strike and at least damage the aircraft carriers before these were capable of attacking the Soviet homeland: a combination of bombers and long-range missiles. The first such missile became the KS-1 Kometa (ASCC/NATO-codename AS-1 Kennel): based on the design of the MiG-15 fighter, it contained a warhead of 800kg and entered service on the Tupolev Tu-4KS heavy bomber (a replica of the Boeing B-29 Superfortress, codenamed Bull by the ASCC/NATO) in 1953. Over the following years, improved designs emerged in the form of the ever bigger and faster K-10, K-16, and KSR-2 anti-ship missiles, mostly equipped with semi-active or active radar homing systems, and primarily deployed from the Tupolev Tu-16 family of bombers (ASCC/NATO-codename Badger). While not optimal for the purpose, the Tu-16 played a crucial role in the further development of the Soviet anti-carrier doctrine, which – gradually – moved from low-altitude to high-altitude approach, because this offered advantage in regards of fuel consumption, longer radar detection ranges, and longer missile range.

During the 1960s, the Soviets found themselves facing the next hurdle in the form of significantly improved airborne early warning (AEW) aircraft of the USN, combined with ever faster, missile-armed interceptors: practically overnight these made all the available bomber and anti-ship missile types obsolete. The solution was to develop supersonic bombers equipped with supersonic missiles. Thus came into being the Tupolev Tu-22 (ASCC/NATO-codename Blinder), which could reach almost Mach 2, and the corresponding K-22 weapon system, the spearhead of which was the Kh-22 anti-ship missile (ASCC/NATO-codename AS-4 Kitchen). Further development of the two led to the entirely new Tupolev Tu-22M family of supersonic bombers (ASCC/NATO-codename Backfire). The Tu-22M-2/3 especially – which was capable of carrying up to three Kh-22MA missiles over a range of up to 3,000km (1,620nm) – was to represent the primary threat for USN carrier battle groups in the late 1970s and through all of the 1980s. Because the Kh-22 was too big for deployment from the Tu-16, around the same time this type was re-equipped with the smaller KSR-5 (ASCC/NATO-codename AS-6 Kingfish).

During this period, another major adaptation of the Soviet tactics for anti-carrier operations was introduced: while at earlier times the Naval Aviation envisaged deploying one or two regiments for an attack on a single CVBG, by the 1980s this was deemed insufficient. Correspondingly, the Soviets devised a new doctrine, under which an entire air division – of two or three regiments – and then two divisions (about 100 aircraft in total) would be deployed to

A Tupolev Tu-22M-2 bomber of the Soviet Naval Aviation, intercepted by the Swedish Air Force in the early 1980s. The inset shows a Kh-22M missile ('AS-4 Kitchen') installed in the ventral hold of the bomber. At 11 metres length and almost six tonnes in weight, Kitchen was a huge weapon: it could carry a conventional warhead of more than 1,000kg, or a 22kT nuclear warhead, at Mach 3 over a range of 400km (216nm) – exactly what the Soviets considered necessary to penetrate defences and at least disable an aircraft carrier. (Swedish Air Force)

The Tu-16 could not pack the hefty Kh-22, and thus required a scaled-down variant: thus came into being the KSR-5 ('AS-6 Kingfish'), one of which is visible in this photograph suspended under the wing of a Tu-16 bomber in the 1980s. Like the Kh-22, the KSR-5 had inertial guidance, with optional mid-course update via a data-link, and terminal active radar homing. It flew at a maximum speed of Mach 3.5 and could reach a range of up to 700km (380nm).

Ultimately, the Soviet Naval Aviation – the only branch to train for anti-carrier operations – never reached the strength considered necessary for operations against more than one CVBG in the northern Atlantic and one in the northern Pacific at once. As of the 1980s, Tu-22M-2/3s were operated by the 5th and 57th Air Divisions of the Northern Fleet and 25th and 143rd Air Divisions of the Pacific Fleet of the Soviet Navy. At the time, their primary hope was to penetrate a CVBG's outer air defences with the help of escorts – usually a full regiment of Sukhoi Su-15TM interceptors – which were expected to crowd, perhaps even to overwhelm the USN's interceptors. (Swedish Air Force)

fight just one aircraft carrier. However, the related built-up of two bomber-equipped divisions for operations in the northern Atlantic and the Norwegian Sea, and two others for operations in the northern Pacific was never completed. Moreover, the Soviets were aware that their chances of actually punching through and damaging just one American aircraft carrier with conventionally armed Kh-22s and KSR-5s were minimal at most.

FROM WILDCAT TO INTRUDER

Since the 1930s, the primary designer and manufacturer of fighter aircraft for the US Navy was the Grumman Aircraft Corporation. Situated in Bethpage, New York, it produced the F4F Wildcat that helped stop the Japanese conquest of the Pacific in 1942, and then pursued German U-Boats in the Atlantic. This was followed by the F6F Hellcat, which secured aerial supremacy in the Pacific. Multiple versions of the Grumman F9F Panther dominated the decks of USN aircraft carriers during the Korean War: while slower than the Soviet-made MiG-15, which emerged as an unpleasant surprise during that conflict, they proved capable of matching it. Grumman was exceptionally fast in adapting to early experiences from that conflict: by 1953, the final version of the Panther – the F9F-6 Cougar – was in service, which equalised whatever advantages the Soviet jet might have had. Only a year later, not only did the company flight-test its first attempt at building a 'swing-wing' jet in the form of the XF10F-1 Jaguar, but the Panther's successor, the Grumman F11F Tiger, entered service, offering further improved flight performance.[2]

However, the 1950s were a period when aerospace-related sciences were advancing at an unprecedented speed, and the competition was not sleeping. Another traditional manufacturer of naval aircraft, Vought (subsequently Ling-Temco-Vought, LTV) won the next of the USN's fighter-contests with its F8U Crusader, which offered even higher speed than the F11F. Moreover, McDonnell of Saint Louis – the company that manufactured the first jet fighter for the USN, the short-lived FH Phantom – continued successful improvement of its own family of naval fighters in the form of the F2H Banshee, and then the F3H Demon, the first interceptor for the USN equipped with AAM-N-7 Sidewinder infra-red-homing missiles, and then Raytheon AAM-N-2 Sparrow semi-active radar homing (SARH) air-to-air missiles. Grumman did recover some of its prestige by winning the contracts to design the first all-weather attack aircraft equipped with a computer-supported navigational/attack system for the USN, the A2F (later A-6) Intruder, and a new airborne early warning (AEW) aircraft, the W2F-1 (later E-2A) Hawkeye. However, subsequently the company seemed to be out of the business of building fighters.[3]

FROM DEMON TO PHANTOM

Short of the Crusader entering fleet-wide service and the Intruder's research and development phase, McDonnell-Douglas offered the Navy a revised variant of the F3H: powered by two slim yet powerful General Electric J-79 Engines, the AH-1 was a fighter-bomber armed with four 20mm internal guns, supposed to carry the bomb-load of the famous Boeing B-17 Flying Fortress of the Second World War, but at supersonic speeds. The USN showed no interest until the manufacturer installed a radar and improved AAM-N-6 Sparrow III missiles to create an all-weather fleet defence interceptor instead. Thus came into being the F4H-1 (later F-4B) Phantom II: a big and powerful fighter that broke an entire series of records shortly after entering operational service. Over the following years, the Phantom II provided such superior performance and reliability that it was to crystallise as the leading, and then the only, fighter interceptor in the Navy of the 1960s and the early 1970s. Unsurprisingly, it attracted the attention of the US Air Force, resulting in the emergence of additional variants tailored for land-based missions: by the end of the decade F-4Cs, F-4Ds, F-4Es, and RF-4Cs (an extremely sophisticated reconnaissance version) outnumbered all other types in the USAF inventory. All were heavily engaged in South East Asia and underwent numerous upgrades of their avionics and weapon systems. By the early 1970s, the standard USN variant was the F-4J, equipped with AWG-10 pulse-Doppler radar, more powerful engines and improved aerodynamics, and excellent AIM-9D Sidewinder air-to-air missiles. By this time, the backbone of the USAF was the F-4E, the first (and only) version armed with an internally installed 20mm General Electric M61 Vulcan cannon, in addition to the solid-state APQ-120 radar, improved AIM-7E-2 Sparrow and AIM-9J Sidewinder air-to-air missiles, and early precision guided munition (PGMs). This was subsequently exported to nearly a dozen customers abroad, including Iran.[4]

HORSES FOR COURSES

While the Phantom offered the capability of intercepting Soviet bombers before these could release their cruise missiles from their maximum assessed range of around 200 nautical miles (370km) this performance was primarily dependent on its acceleration and speed, less so on the range of its radar and weaponry. If interceptors were delayed for whatever reason, a CVBG would find itself unprotected. For this reason, and because the

An F-8 Corsair of the US Navy's VF-51 Screaming Eagles squadron, armed with an AIM-9D Sidewinder air-to-air missile, seen next to the fin of a Soviet Tu-16 bomber, high above the Norwegian Sea.

A formation of F3H Demons of the fighter squadron VF-64, seen while assigned to CVW-2 and embarked aboard the USS *Midway*, in the late 1950s. The Demon was the first interceptor of the USN equipped not only with radar, but also with radar-guided missiles, and served as a direct predecessor to the famous F-4 Phantom.

An F-4B from the VF-41 Black Aces, next to a Soviet Tu-95 bomber over the Norwegian Sea in the 1970s.

USN remained insistent on its 'horses for courses' philosophy – in which naval aircraft were closely tailored for a specific mission, instead of having multi-mission capabilities – it continued to search for a superior solution. A suitable weapon – the big Bendix XAAM-N-10 Eagle air-to-air missile with the range of 127 miles (235km) – was ready by 1958, followed by a suitable radar, the pulse-Doppler AN/APQ-81, two years later. However, microtechnology was still in the realms of science fiction and thus both the Eagle missile and the APQ-81 proved too big for installation in any of the available fighter types. The original solution called for the development of the Douglas Model D-766 Missiler, officially designated the F6D: an uninspiring design optimised to carry the heaviest possible air-to-air armament at the expense of performance and agility, envisaged to circle the fleet at slow speed, and – guided by the Hawkeye – lob Eagle air-to-air missiles at incoming Soviet bombers from maximum range. However, not only was the F6D unavailingly compared with the far superior F-4B Phantom, but then the E-2 encountered major development problems and was almost cancelled in 1960. Eventually, the conclusion was obvious: at the time the available fighter jet designs were growing ever bigger and heavier there was ever less space on aircraft carriers to afford the luxury of operating single-mission aircraft: the Missiler was cancelled by the last Secretary of Defence in the outgoing Eisenhower Administration in December 1960.[5]

On 20 January 1961, the administration of President John F Kennedy took office, bringing with it a new Defence Secretary, Robert McNamara – and a new buzzword: commonality. Driven by expected financial advantages in regards of acquisition, support infrastructure and maintenance, McNamara demanded that the US Navy and the USAF develop a common aircraft that was to carry out interception, air superiority, battlefield support, interdiction and reconnaissance missions. The result was the emergence of the General Dynamics F-111, a jet originally envisaged to carry heavy warload at level speed in excess of Mach 2.5 over a range

Artist's conception of the F6D-1 Missiler, the original 'fleet defender' designed to carry the AN/APQ-81 pulse-Doppler radar and XAAM-N-10 Eagle long-range missiles.

One of the F-111B prototypes in flight, with an AIM-54 Phoenix missile just visible on a left underwing pylon.

units. While the AN/APQ-81 was meanwhile further developed into the AN/ASG-18 and then the Hughes Airborne Weapons Group Nine (AN/AWG-9) radars, and the XAAM-N-10 Eagle into the highly-promising AIM-47 Falcon and then the AIM-54 Phoenix missiles, all were very expensive and foremost meant to be used against Soviet bombers equipped with cruise missiles. On the contrary, the Vietnam War showed that the idea of all-missile fighters was not viable, and any new fighter would have to be able to fight close-in air combats with guns. While weapons-related problems could be solved by their further development, most of the other issues could not: plagued by its high weight and a mass of other problems, the F-111B was refused further funding by the US Congress, and then terminated in December 1968. The US Navy was now in urgent need of a new fleet defender – one not only capable of intercepting future Soviet supersonic bombers and their hypersonic anti-ship missiles, but also of engaging small and nimble 'MiGs' in air combat.

GRUMMAN'S LAST CAT

In the present day, the development of any new combat aircraft regularly lasts in excess of 20 years, easily gulps up to US$1 trillion, and employs entire 'armies' of highly-qualified civilian and military experts. The reasons are … 'complex' – and, in addition to the purpose of securing the status and income of all the involved corporations (and jobs of their employees), primarily related to the fact that the enterprises involved in this business and the military services seeking to procure resulting aircraft are trying to predict the future of warfare – including possible future threats – for the full projected life-span of the new aircraft: for the next 30 to 50 years. Ironically, and as described above, in the case of the F-14, the threat perception and the resulting requirements were already existent and well-known, even if – as it was to become known only much later – based on rather exaggerated 'worst case scenarios'. Moreover, the primary weapon system was already available and 'waiting' for a suitable platform. Unsurprisingly, the research and development of the Tomcat took less than three years.

Certainly enough, it was already in 1965 that, spurred by F-111B's problems, the USN requested Grumman to study a design for an advanced air superiority fighter. After examining more

of 1,475km (800nm). However, although eventually developed into a highly successful, low-altitude/high-speed, all weather and night (AWX) nuclear and precision-strike platform for the USAF, the version developed for the USN, the F-111B proved ill-suited for carrier operations. Heavily loaded with advanced avionics and being the first swing wing design to enter series production in the USA, its development was protracted while gulping taxpayers' money without an end. Meanwhile, the USA became involved in the Second Vietnam War, and Phantoms found themselves fighting small and nimble MiG-17s in 1964, followed by MiG-21s in 1966. The Navy's first combat experiences quickly showed that, entirely preoccupied with preparations for fighting an all-out nuclear war against the USSR and allies, not only had its aviators lost their skills in fighting air combats, but that their Phantoms were ill-equipped for this discipline: their Sidewinder and Sparrow missiles underwent insufficient and unrealistic testing before service entry, and then against only non-manoeuvring targets; they proved extremely sensitive to improper handling, and their effective deployment in combat depended on the kind of skill not available in operational than 6,000 configurations, Grumman reduced these to a handful collectively known as Project 303. While even bigger than the F-4 Phantom, this was equipped with a modified AWG-9 but, contrary to popular belief, was no 'pure fleet defence interceptor': rather an air superiority fighter capable of outmanoeuvring MiG-17s and MiG-21s, with AIM-7 Sparrow missiles as its primary armament. Only once this capability was achieved, did Grumman's engineers sit back to figure out how to screw six AIM-54s onto it – without spoiling the basic fighter role.

Little happened before Congress stopped funding the F-111B in May 1968. Wasting no time, only two months later the USN issued a Request for Proposal to industry, demanding a two-seat, twin-engined fighter jet incorporating the AWG-9 radar, AIM-54, AIM-7, and AIM-9 missiles, and also an integral 20mm General Electric M61A Vulcan cannon. In addition to Grumman, General Dynamics, LTV, McDonnell-Douglas and North American-Rockwell promptly submitted their proposals: on 14 January 1969 the Pentagon selected Grumman's 303E design and contracted the company for six research, development, and evaluation aircraft and 463 production examples under the designation F-14 for service with the USN and US Marine Corps (USMC). The contract further stipulated the first flight to take on or before 31 January 1971. Highly confident about prospects for success, Grumman pre-ordered the fabrication of various assemblies before December 1968 and was thus able to react very quickly. Indeed, by 1970 it adapted the original 303E to meet various Navy demands – like replacement of the single vertical tail by two (to improve directional stability in the event of engine failure at high speed), and the removal of two ventral folding fins – and prepared the first prototype: nick-named the 'Tomcat', this made its maiden flight on 21 December 1970.[6]

An F-14A of VF-2 Bounty Hunters, about to be launched from USS *Enterprise* (CVN-65), during a deployment off Vietnam, on 15 March 1975.

An F-14A of VF-1 Wolfpack, escorting two Tu-16PP reconnaissance bombers of the Soviet Naval Aviation over the north-western Pacific, in the mid-1980s.

ENGINE PROBLEMS

Even once Grumman had secured the contract for the F-14, the battle for survival of the entire program was far from over: now the company faced the tremendous task of launching series production of what by the time was the – by far – most complex and most expensive fighter jet ever manufactured. The Navy's original intention was to acquire 61 F-14As powered by the Pratt & Whitney TF-30-P-412 engine (essentially the same powerplant as that of the stillborn F-111B), before switching to the definitive F-14B model that was to be powered by the new, Advanced Technology Engine (ATE) still undergoing development. Although meanwhile a mature design the TF-30 proved ill-suited for service on the F-14 soon after the type passed its initial operational evaluation with the USN's test and evaluation squadron VX-4 in 1973. The core problem was that it was never designed for stress caused by close-in air combat, where pilots tended to rapidly switch power back and forward or engage and disengage afterburner in a matter of seconds. The TF-30 began suffering numerous component failures, the most frequent of which – and always the most dangerous – were failures of the fan blades: whenever these occurred, the broken blades scythed through everything in their path, including fuel lines and tanks, causing catastrophic fires. This was the kind of problem for which no solution was in sight because the ATE – in the form of the Pratt & Whitney F401-PW-400 – proved a non-starter, and was cancelled in April 1974. Thus, the Navy was forced to continue ordering TF-30-powered F-14As while launching a programme of fixes for an engine that simply could not do the job. None proved satisfactory and engine-related issues were to cost the service dearly. Not only were about 80 F-14s to crash during the 1970s and the 1980s, mostly due to engine-related issues, but ultimately the programme of fixes that resulted in the relatively reliable TF-30-P414/414As that emerged in the mid-1980s, cost the USN more than the development of an entirely new engine.[7]

LIFE-SAVING EXPORT TO IRAN

Meanwhile, escalating costs of the entire F-14-program and engine-related problems were an opportunity upon which multiple detractors seized. In August 1974, Congress voted to cut off the Navy loan that financed Grumman, and thus stop the entire F-14 program. Ironically, by that time Grumman had secured an export order – to a country nowadays nobody in the USA would consider selling a weapon system to as advanced as the Tomcat was as of the time: Iran. Following extensive evaluation and a fly-out against the brand-new McDonnell-Douglas F-15A Eagle, in August 1973 the government in Tehran reached the decision to place an order for F-14As. The US Government granted its approval in November of the same year, and the first contract for 30 Tomcats was signed in January 1974; the second, for 50 additional jets followed in June of the same year. Contrary to the US Congress, the Imperial Iranian Air Force (IIAF) was firmly determined to get its Tomcats. Thus, when the law-makers in Washington decided to *de-facto* force Grumman into bankruptcy, Shah Reza Pahlavi II of Iran ordered the Bank Mehli to step into the breach with a loan that credited Grumman to manufacture F-14s for the IIAF. This not only encouraged further investors, but eventually forced Congress to reverse its decision and continue buying Tomcats for the US Navy.[8]

DEPLOYMENT

Not only Grumman, but also thousands of officers of the USN became involved in getting the F-14 into operational service. In August 1972, VF-124 Gunfighters was commissioned at the Naval Air Station (NAS) Miramar as the first unit to become equipped with F-14s: the squadron was to serve as the training unit for more than the next 30 years. The first fleet squadrons to be equipped with the Tomcat were VF-1 Wolfpack and VF-2 Bounty Hunters, officially activated on 14 October 1972, before undergoing an 18-month conversion course with VF-124. Delivery of their aircraft lasted from 31 October 1973 until 26 April 1974 and, once their work-ups and carrier qualifications were completed, the two units joined the Carrier Air Wing 14 (CVW-14) to embark the nuclear-powered aircraft carrier USS *Enterprise* (CVN-65) for a deployment to the western Pacific and Indian Ocean, starting from 17 September 1974. Next, two F-4-units – VF-14 Tophatters and VF-32 Swordsmen – completed their conversion courses and deployed with CVW-1

TABLE 1: F-14, OPERATIONAL DEPLOYMENT WITH US NAVY, 1974-1999			
SQUADRON	FIRST DEPLOYMENT	FIRST CARRIER AIR WING (TAILCODE)	NOTES
VF-1 Wolfpack	Sep 1974	CVW-14 (NK)	to CVW-2 (NE) in 1980; disestablished 1993
VF-2 Bounty Hunters	Sep 1974	CVW-14 (NK)	to CVW-2 (NE) in 1980; to F-14D in 1993
VF-14 Tophatters	Jun 1975	CVW-1 (AB)	to CVW-6 (AE) in 1982, to CVW-3 (AC) in 1983
VF-32 Swordsmen	Jun 1975	CVW-1 (AB)	to CVW-6 (AE) in 1982, to CVW-3 (AC) in 1983
VF-142 Ghostriders	Apr 1976	CVW-6 (AE)	to CVW-7 (AG) in 1979; to F-14A+ in 1989; disestablished in 1995
VF-143 Pukin' Dogs	Apr 1976	CVW-6 (AE)	to CVW-7 (AG) in 1979; to F-14A+ in 1989
VF-24 Checkertails	Apr 1977	CVW-9 (NG)	renamed Renegades; to F-14A+ in 1989
VF-211 Checkmates	Apr 1977	CVW-9 (NG)	to F-14A+ in 1989
VF-114 Aardvarks	Oct 1977	CVW-11 (NH)	disestablished in 1993
VF-213 Black Lions	Oct 1977	CVW-11 (NH)	to F-14D in 1997
VF-41 Black Aces	Dec 1977	CVW-8 (AJ)	
VF-84 Jolly Rogers	Dec 1977	CVW-8 (AJ)	disestablished in 1995
VF-51 Screaming Eagles	May 1979	CVW-15 (NL)	disestablished in 1995
VF-111 Sundowners	May 1979	CVW-15 (NL)	disestablished in 1995
VF-11 Red Rippers	Jan 1982	CVW-3 (AC)	to CVW-6 (AE) in 1983; to F-14D in 1992
VF-31 Tomcatters	Jan 1982	CVW-3 (AC)	to CVW-6 (AE) in 1983; to F-14D in 1992
VF-102 Diamondbacks	May 1982	CVW-1 (AB)	to F-14B in 1994
VF-33 Tarsiers	May 1982	CVW-1 (AB)	re-named Starfighters in 1985; disestablished in 1993
VF-74 Bedevilers	Jun 1983	CVW-17 (AA)	to F-14A+ in 1988
VF-103 Sluggers	Jun 1983	CVW-17 (AA)	to F-14A+ in 1988
VF-154 Black Knights	Feb 1985	CVW-14 (NK)	to CVW-5 (NF) in 1991; disestablished in 1996
VF-21 Freelancers	Feb 1985	CVW-14 (NK)	to CVW-5 (NF) in 1991; disestablished in 1996
VF-191 Satan's Kittens	Oct 1987	CVW-10 (NM)	disestablished in 1988
VF-194 Red Lightnings	Oct 1987	CVW-10 (NM)	disestablished in 1988

TABLE 2: AIRWINGS AND AIRCRAFT CARRIERS OF THE USN, 1987-1991

AIRWING	TAILCODE	CARRIER
CVW-1	AB	USS *America* (CV-66)
CVW-2	NE	USS *Constellation* (CV-63)
CVW-3	AC	USS *John F Kennedy* (CV-67)
CVW-5	NF	USS *Midway* (CV-41)
CVW-6	AE	USS *Forrestal* (CV-59)
CVW-7	AG	USS *Dwight D Eisenhower* (CVN-68)
CVW-8	AJ	USS *Nimitz* (CVN-68), to USS *Theodore Roosevelt* (CVN-71) in 1988
CVW-9	NG	USS *Kitty Hawk* (CV-63), to USS *Nimitz* (CVN-68) in 1988
CVW-10	NM	working up for USS *Abraham Lincoln* (CVN-72)
CVW-11	NH	USS *Enterprise* (CVN-65)
CVW-14	NK	USS *Constellation* (CV-64), to USS *Independence* (CV-62) in 1988
CVW-15	NL	USS *Carl Vinson* (CVN-70)
CVW-16	AH	planned for USS *George Washington* (CVN-73) in 1991-1992
CVW-17	AA	USS *Saratoga* (CV-60)

aboard USS *John F Kennedy* (CV-67) for a Mediterranean cruise, starting on 28 June 1975.[9]

As ever additional Tomcats rolled off the production line, six former F-4 squadrons and two former F-8 squadrons converted to the type in the 1974-1977 period (see Table 1 for details), prompting the USN into establishing its second training unit: VF-101 Grim Reapers at NAS Oceana, on the Atlantic Coast, officially commissioned in July 1977. Subsequent build-up was seriously troubled by engine-related issues and lack of spares, which caused the fleet to be grounded several times. As a consequence, another two units completed their conversion courses only in 1979: there followed a gap of no less than three years until the first out of eight additional ex-F-4 squadrons was declared operational on the Tomcat in 1982. Eventually, the process of replacing the remaining Phantoms lasted into 1985, by when two reserve units re-equipped with the type, and the Navy launched the work on re-establishing two regular squadrons for its planned 16th aircraft carrier – an idea that was cancelled in the spring of 1988.[10]

TOMCAT SUPREME

The capability offered by service entry of the F-14 far surpassed the significance of 'introducing a new fighter aircraft': it propelled Navy's Tomcat's squadrons into a position of dominating the aerial warfare of the late 1970s and all of the 1980s. The principal reason for this was a weapon system that – even if centred on a much upgraded version of a radar originally developed in the late 1950s and the early 1960s – was still ahead of its time and easily outmatched nearly everything available anywhere else. Its core was the AWG-9 radar and fire-control system that, from the front towards the rear, included a total of 27 units, starting with the planar-array radar antenna with 91.4cm (36in) diameter, an antenna controller, synchronisers, microwave circuits and Doppler clutter processors, digital computers, fire control system, cockpit displays, and two data-links. The installation of all this equipment into a single aircraft was possible due to huge advances in the design of radars and computers during the 1960s: while still an analogue system, the AWG-9 incorporated the second generation of solid-state technology including throughput processors, coherent transmitters and amplifiers, microprocessors (necessary to filter ground clutter and enable tracking of low-flying targets), entirely new tracking algorithms, and was capable of emitting at a new, high

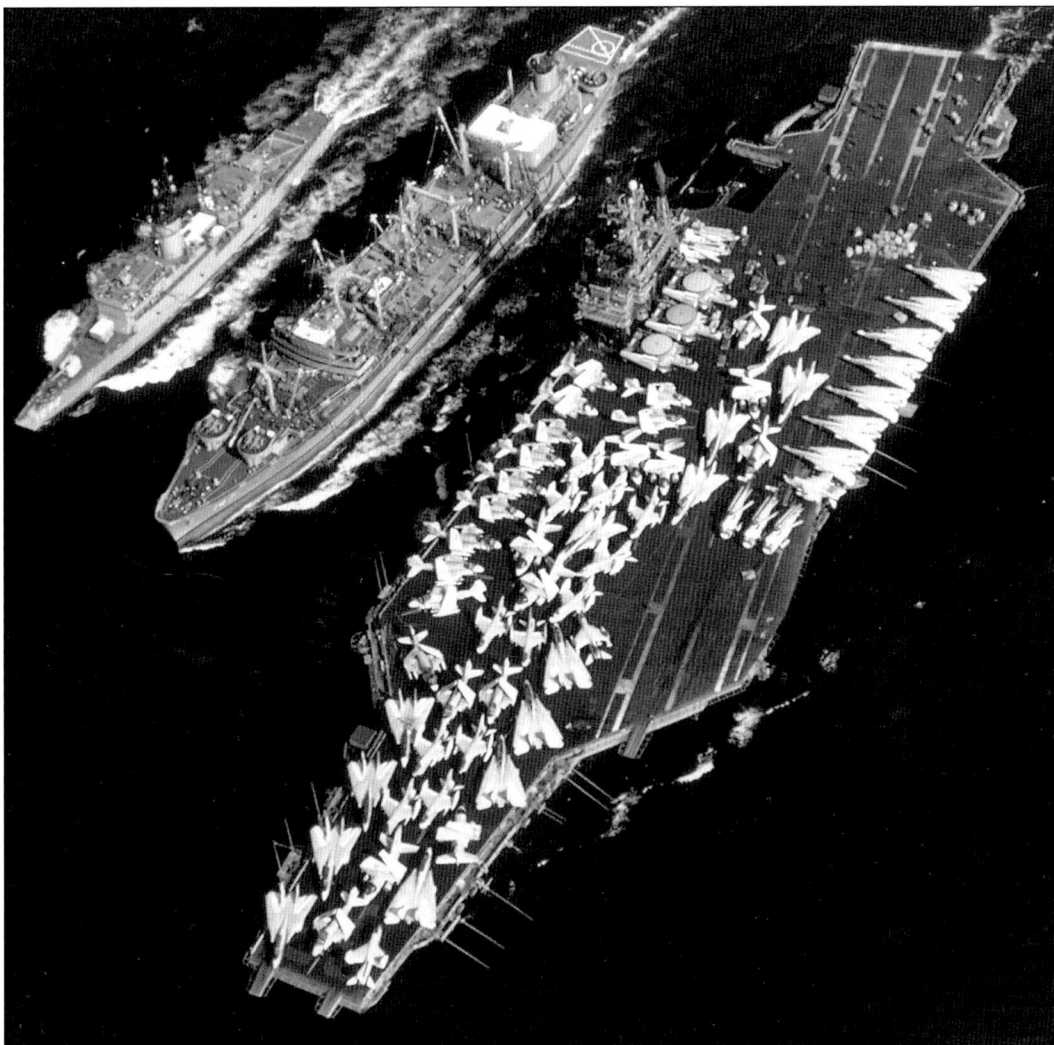

Aircraft carrier USS *John F Kennedy* with brand-new F-14As of CVW-1 on deck, seen during an underway replenishment operation in the Mediterranean Sea in 1975.

Tactical Information Display (TID) in the rear cockpit of an F-14A, showing the radar picture as presented by the AWG-9 in the TWS mode. In this case, the scope was set to a range of 25 nautical miles. (Lt Gerald B Parsons, USN/Defenseimagery)

pulse repetition frequency (essential for ultra-long-range detection capability). The peak output was 10.2kW, which made it the most powerful airborne intercept radar in operational service on combat aircraft until the service entry of the Lockheed F-22 Raptor equipped with the APG-77, in 2005.[11]

The AWG-9 was extremely versatile: it had six basic working modes (four of which were pulse-Doppler), with 19 transmission channels for pulse-Doppler search signals, of which 6 were for guidance of AIM-54 missiles, and 5 for AIM-7s. The longest-ranged working mode was the Pulse-Doppler-Search (PDS), which offered the ability to detect bomber-sized targets from as far as 277km (150nm) and fighter-sized targets (radar cross section of less than 5 square metres, like the MiG-21) from 213km (115nm). The Pulse-Doppler Single Target Track (PDSTT) mode was used for long-range AIM-54 shots and for attacks on targets emitting strong electronic countermeasures (ECM), but could also be deployed to guide AIM-7 Sparrows out to a range of 70km (38nm) or AIM-9 Sidewinders out to a range of 16km (10nm). Perhaps the most important was the Track-While-Scan (TWS) mode, in which the AWG-9 had a maximum detection range of 166km (90nm), but could scan immense volumes of airspace (about 15 times more than best system ever installed into the F-4) while simultaneously tracking up to 24 targets – six of which could be engaged with AIM-54 missiles at the same time. All of these working modes enabled look-down/shoot down engagements (i.e. targeting of objects operating at very low altitudes): moreover, when working in the TWS mode, the AWG-9's emissions were difficult to identify for contemporary radar warning receivers, and thus warning of an attack was minimal – if there was any.

While most of these working modes could be used for setting up attacks in which the fire-control system was selecting targets and releasing AIM-54s on its own – indeed: in automatic mode – the AWG-9 retained its 'old school', man-in-the-loop pulse radar modes, enabling the radar intercept officer (RIO) in the rear cockpit to 'manually' pick up weak radar returns out to the range of 91km (49nm) in Single Target Track – or 115km (62nm) in Pulse Search mode. Finally, the radar had three air-combat modes (Pilot Lock on, Manual Rapid Lock on and Vertical Scan Lock on), enabling the crew – foremost the pilot – to quickly lock on to targets engaged in close-in air combat at ranges out to 9.23km (9nm).

An AIM-54 missile seen shortly after release: when underway over long range, the missile first climbed to a high altitude. Its big size, weight and speed earned it the nickname 'Buffalo'. (USN)

Weapon firing was performed by a separate fire-control computer, the AWG-15, while the problems inherent in using four different weapons in rapid succession and without particular order were solved by using an integrated armament control system. Alternatively, all the weapon options could be pre-programmed and stored prior to take-off, in which case every weapon was instantly prepared for launch at the touch of a switch.

HELPING HANDS

While a massive improvement over anything operated at earlier times, the Navy never envisaged operating its F-14s entirely on their own: rather as a part of an entire air warfare system, the pinnacle of which was to become an airborne early warning (AEW) aircraft. The original idea for AEW was relatively simple and emerged in Great Britain during the early 1940s. The range of ground-

The dramatic sight of an AIM-54 approaching a hard-turning QF-4 target drone (left) – and detonating directly below it – during a test shot in 1983.

based radars was limited and disturbed by the terrain: thus, the idea was born to install them on aircraft and thus to significantly improve their range and enable detection beyond the horizon. Of course, realising all of this proved to be a much troublesome issue and thus it was only in the early 1960s that the first modern AEW aircraft emerged in the form of the above-mentioned Grumman E-2 Hawkeye. Certainly enough, even the E-2A was nothing but trouble early on. It experienced so many problems that its production was stopped until further work was completed and the new E-2B emerged in 1964. The definitive variant, the E-2C, was first-flown in 1971, and introduced to service two years later. While this glider-like, turboprop-powered aircraft was slow, it could operate at altitudes of up to 9,144m (30,000ft), from where its AN/APS-120 radar could pick up targets with an RCS of only 1 square metre from as far as 222km (119nm). Subsequent sub-variants received ever more sophisticated radars and advanced computers, and an identification friend or foe (IFF) interrogator, which enabled it to simultaneously track up to 300, and then 3,000 targets over ever longer ranges, to identify them, and to indicate their position, speed, and height.[12]

A pair of E-2Cs of Airborne Early Warning Squadron 124 (VAW-124), embarked with CVW-8 aboard USS *Nimitz* (CVN-68): the squadron earned itself the nickname 'Bear Aces' for its numerous intercepts of Soviet Tu-95s off Iceland, in December 1980. (USN)

A belly view at an F-14A of the VF-111 Sundowners armed with an AIM-54A Phoenix missile. (USN)

For cooperation with the F-14, the E-2C was equipped with the Link 4 datalink, capable of downloading the Hawkeye's radar picture to the TID in the rear cockpit of the Tomcat. Later on, starting in 1990, Navy Tomcats were equipped with the upgraded ASW-27C Link 4A, which enabled up to four Tomcats to communicate securely with each other. Certainly enough, the two datalinks could not be used simultaneously: nevertheless, they offered immense advantages in regards of increasing the situational awareness of the Tomcat's crew – especially in complex tactical situations. By downloading the radar picture directly from the mission computer of an E-2C in real time, the RIO did not need to power up the AWG-9, and thus even the Tomcat's presence was likely to remain unknown to the enemy. Alternatively, four RIOs could exchange their radar pictures and thus have cooperative engagement capability. The overall result was a great expansion of the possible battlespace, of maximum detection and engagement ranges, increased time for the crew and weapon systems to react, and improvement in target tracking continuity and accuracy – and all of that 30 years before such performances became a 'norm' for other fighter interceptors.[13]

The effectiveness of the E-2C supported F-14A was put to extensive test during the above-mentioned Mediterranean Sea deployment by USS *Kennedy* in 1975. During exercises with the Spanish air force, USAF units stationed in Spain, and the Turkish, Italian, and French air forces, the combination of a Hawkeye and Tomcat proved vastly superior to whatever came their way. For example, during the Exercise Corsair (USN designation) or LaFayette (French designation), in December 1975, the French air force launched 91 simulated strike sorties with its Dassault Mirage IIIs (loaded with Martel anti-radar missiles) from Escadron de Chasse (EC) 1/3 Champagne, deployed at Base Aérienne 126 Solenzara in Corsica, and Super Mystère B.2s from EC.1/12 Cambréesis from BA.125 Isres, near Marseille (62 sorties). Three Mirage IIIRDs provided tactical reconnaissance for strike operations of the fighter-bombers. Tomcats from VF-14 and VF-32 successfully intercepted every single one, and even the French air force's assessment pointed out that 'more than half have been thwarted' by the F-14/E-2-team.[14]

SORTING OUT THE MUSCLE JET

Despite the overall success of the F-14 and its weapon systems, through all of the 1970s the 1980s, Tomcat continued suffering from engine and handling-related issues. While having perfectly practical consequences, the question of replacing engines was foremost one of politics, management, and funding – and something the USN took years to overcome. In 1981, complaints from the fleet prompted the Navy to pull out the sole prototype of the still-born F-14B from long-term storage, re-equip it with two General Electric F-101-DFE engines, and launch a new series of flight-tests. The result was a spectacular increase in thrust, a sparkling improvement

2
OPPOSING FORCES

As often the case with the Cold War, a major battle between the USN's CVBGs and the bombers of the Soviet Naval Aviation never took place. Instead, American-operated F-14s became involved in several skirmishes at various spots around the Mediterranean Sea during the 1980s. Moreover, their primary opponents of the 1987-1999 period were not Tupolev-designed bombers, but much smaller interceptors of Mikoyan i Gurevich or Sukhoi design, many of which experienced their own, and as many, if not bigger, problems than the USN experienced when pressing the F-14 into service.

To understand what was going on in the USSR in this regard, it is important to keep in mind that ever since 1935, the main commanding, administrative and supervising body of the Soviet armed forces was the General Staff of the Armed Forces of the USSR (GenStab). The GenStab was both, a de-facto branch of its own within the armed forces and the 'jointness' element: a caste of top military theoreticians drawn from all branches, responsible for converting political orders into military theory – and thus also for all the decision-making in regards of how to equip and train the Soviet armed forces. In its supervising position, the GenStab was responsible for writing threat perceptions on the basis of which all weapon systems and all military equipment – from spades and gas masks, to fighter jets and intercontinental ballistic missiles – were designed, not only in the USSR, but in the countries of the WTO: the GenStab were the famous 'Soviet military theoreticians' frequently quoted, but rarely named in related Western reports.

SOVIET REQUIREMENTS

According to the theories of the GenStab in the 1940s and the 1950s, the ultimate form of a war between NATO and the WTO was an all-out nuclear conflict in which the Soviets would face thousands of bombers armed with nuclear bombs. Correspondingly, this form of warfare was assigned top priority and the USSR invested heavily into research, development and production of a radar network covering the whole of Soviet airspace, and then into new interceptors and ground-based air defence systems. The result was a specialised (and independent) branch of the armed forces responsible for this task – the Anti-Air Defence Troops or the Air Defence Command (*Protivovozdushnaya Oborona Strany*, PVO) – that experienced a rapid growth. While capable of only providing high-altitude radar coverage over the most important urban centres of the European part of the USSR, and regularly failing to intercept Western reconnaissance aircraft operating at high altitudes deep inside Soviet airspace all through the 1950s, during the following decade the PVO essentially sealed the entire Soviet airspace by deploying multiple integrated air defence systems (IADS) comprising early warning radars, manned fighter-interceptors, and surface-to-air missiles (SAMs).

Realising this, Western strategists were quick in adapting their planning. Henceforth, ballistic missiles took over the role of the primary means of delivery of nuclear warheads, while bombers operated by the Strategic Air Command of the USAF, and the Bomber Command of the RAF were expected to fly ever faster and higher, and were re-armed with guided air-to-surface missiles, enabling them to deploy their nuclear bombs from outside the range of the Soviet air defences. Simultaneously, NATO opted to re-arm most of its air forces with the Lockheed F-104G Starfighter armed with US-made B-43 tactical nuclear weapons, while the USAF introduced to service the even more powerful Republic

VF-142 and VF-143 were the third and fourth units to convert to the F-14A+ in 1989. Both squadrons were embarked aboard USS *Eisenhower* (CVN-69) during Operation Desert Shield in 1990. (USN)

in performance, and an enormous increase in reliability. Still, the program was once again cancelled and, one year later, an entirely new project designated F-14D initiated: it was only within this framework that the decision was taken to re-engine the surviving F-14As with the General Electric F110-GE-400 engines. The result was what the Navy designated the F-14A+ (re-designated as the F-14B in May 1991), deliveries of which began in 1987.[15]

As well as the stall-prone TF-30s, another major issue was handling problems. Because as of the late 1960s there were no computers to automatically trim the aircraft for the pilot, the F-14 was the last US fighter jet without the fly-by-wire (FBW) control system: the last still flown, literally, 'by hand'. While a very stable and forgiving aircraft, it had its vices like susceptibility to wing-rock on take-offs, to Dutch-rolls, adverse sideslips on landing, and flat spins. As of the 1980s, no cure had been found: indeed, it would be only during the mid-1990s that the British company GEC-Marconi Avionics developed the Digital Flight Control System (DFCS) for the F-14: derived from the fly-by-wire computers developed for the Eurofighter EF-2000 Typhon II, installed from 1998, and in fleet-wide service by 2000, the DFCS aided handling and performance throughout the flight envelope. Combined with new engines, it completely revamped the combat performance of what was meanwhile a 30-year-old design.

F-105 Thunderchief, capable of reaching supersonic speeds while underway at very low altitudes. This left the Soviets confronted with literally thousands of nuclear-armed bombers and fighter-bombers. Obviously, when fighting such a war there was no margin for error: all such bombers and fighter-bombers had to be intercepted and destroyed within the shortest possible period of time, with precise blows. This in turn required a tightly integrated and centralised IADS, controlled by one central command node, capable of ascertaining reliable interception and destruction of thousands of different targets through coordinating the efforts of thousands of their own interceptors (manned or not). Moreover, manned interceptors deployed by such an IADS had to be brought to the point: they had to be easy to manufacture, maintain and operate in large numbers, while not supposed to waste time by flying combat air patrols (CAPs), nor expected to last for more than 200 hours of combat operations. Although as of 1960 both the PVO and the Soviet Tactical Aviation (*Frontovaya Aviatsiya*, FA) were in the process of introducing to service precisely such new interceptors in the form of the Sukhoi Su-9 and MiG-21, respectively, it was already clear that both lacked the capabilities necessary to effectively combat all the future threats. Correspondingly, between 1959 and 1963, the GenStab issued requirements for several new tactical interceptors. All were to emphasise speed – in climb and in level flight – and to carry powerful weapon systems: one project, designed to catch high and fast-flying strategic bombers and reconnaissance aircraft, eventually received the designation MiG-25; the other, designed to catch low-flying F-104s, F-105s, and F-111s, eventually crystallised as the MiG-23.

With the USSR lacking the necessary technologies and know-how, and the GenStab modifying its requirements several times, the development of both types experienced several delays. For example, the prototype of the future MiG-23 in its final form was first flown in 1967, but the type entered production only three years later. Moreover, because the research and development of its weapon system was lagging behind the development of the aircraft, the first few dozens of early MiG-23s were rolled out from the factory still lacking the planned radars and weapons.

FLOGGER

Despite their imposing performances in speed (both new MiGs were clearly superior to the F-14 in regards of their thrust-to-weight ratio and speed in climb) – the new Soviet fighter-interceptors had one thing in common: because the USSR was lagging vis-à-vis the West in the development of advanced and miniaturised technologies, their avionics-outfits were rather austere. To a certain degree, this was a logical decision: operations against their ultimate targets – whether high or low-flying carriers of nuclear bombs – foremost required a very fast response, an interceptor that was to be vectored very precisely, and a weapon system granting the capability to shoot down its target with a single blow. Furthermore, the kind of avionics installed into the F-14 was neither available nor affordable for the USSR. Instead, the Soviets opted to install their few available computers into the headquarters of their IADS, rather than into aircraft. As a result, both the MiG-23 (ASCC/NATO-codename 'Flogger') and MiG-25 (ASCC/NATO-codename 'Foxbat') required the support of a well-developed network of radar stations, intelligence-gathering stations, and ground-control systems for effective operations.

As the research and design of the MiG-23 and MiG-25 progressed, combat experiences with the MiG-21 from the wars

A pair of early MiG-23Ms of the Soviet Air Force. Because the development of the avionics for this type lagged behind that of the airframe, both were initially armed with older, shorter-ranged weapons: in this case with nearly useless R-3S (AA-2 Atoll) air-to-air missiles. (US DoD)

A Soviet MiG-23MLD forward deployed at Cam Ranh air base in Vietnam in 1987-1988, seen after being intercepted by an F-14A of the USN. The MiG-23MLD was the ultimate interceptor version of this prolific family. (USN)

in the Middle East and Vietnam of the late 1960s indicated that the work on future fighter jets in the USSR was heading in the wrong direction. Unsurprisingly, when first MiG-23s reached trial and evaluation units of the Soviet Air Force (*Voyenno-Vozdushnye Sily*, VVS) Soviet test pilots were disappointed: they would have preferred a 'longer-ranged, heavier armed' MiG-21. However, in the Soviet hierarchy nobody dared to explain to the GenStab that its basic ideas could be wrong, or that it had wasted a dozen years developing a weapon system that was obsolete at its service entry. Instead, the MiG-23 was rushed into mass production and the designer then spent the next dozen years refining it. The result was the emergence of an entire family of fighter-interceptors and fighter-bombers, the first of which lacked not only an effective weapon system but also manoeuvrability, and suffered from poor manufacturing quality. Nevertheless, thousands of MiG-23s were pressed into service with the VVS/FA and the PVO during the first half of the 1970s, and hundreds were exported – especially to the Middle East. Rather unsurprisingly, they quickly earned themselves a very poor reputation.

Eventually, after the short-lived MiG-23 and MiG-23S, the much-improved MiG-23M was first-flown in 1972: as well as including an improved engine and wing-design, it was the first armed with the full S-23 weapon system, including the Sapfir-23D-III radar, and the TP-23 infra-red search and track system (IRST). On its service entry in 1974, the MiG-23M's primary armament consisted of two big R-23 air-to-air missiles (ASCC/NATO-codename 'AA-7 Apex'), which had a maximum engagement range of 26km (14nm), and R-13M (ASCC/NATO-codename 'AA-2D Atoll') short-range infra-red homing missiles. The R-23 was available in two variants: the semi-active radar homing (SARH) R-23R and the infra-red homing R-23T.[1]

FOXBAT

The situation was only a notch better in regards of the MiG-25. First-flown in 1964, its first interceptor variant – MiG-25P – entered service in 1972 following protracted test and evaluation. Contrary to the MiG-23, this received a fully developed avionics suite right from the start, including the RP-25 Smerch-A I-band, low-PRF pulse radar that, while completely lacking the look-down/shoot-down capability, was a powerful (peak output was 600kW) and jamming-resistant system optimised for detecting and attacking high and fast-flying bombers. While possessing a maximal theoretical detection range out to 100km (54nm), the Smerch was actually optimised for operations in the face of massive electronic countermeasures (ECM). Moreover, the jet was armed with four huge R-40 air-to-air missiles (ASCC/NATO-codename 'AA-6 Acrid') optimised to deliver fatal blows against large targets in the thin air at high altitudes, where the effects of their warheads would be quickly dissipated. These were available in two variants: R-40R (SARH) and R-40T (infra-red homing), which – depending on the engagement mode – had a maximum engagement range of between 35 and 50km (19-27nm).[2]

In the late 1960s and early 1970s, wild rumours about the MiG-25 were making circles in the West, causing an outright shock. Early intelligence reports not only mixed it with the MiG-23, but insisted on a top operational speed of Mach 3+ – although this was actually possible only at the risk of significant damage to the engines and the aircraft. Moreover, the MiG-25 was misunderstood as an extremely sophisticated, agile fighter, largely manufactured of titanium and designed for air combat. It was only when PVO pilot Viktor Belenko defected to Japan flying a MiG-25P in September 1976 that the West obtained a better understanding of the type. Namely, an inspection of Belenko's aircraft by specialists of the Foreign Technologies Division (FTD) of the USAF revealed that the MiG-25 was manufactured in a very conventional fashion. It was largely made from nickel-steel alloys welded by hand (and thus very heavy), it was stressed for accelerations up to 4.5g (and thus ill-suited for close-in air combat), and its avionics were based on vacuum-tube technology at least a generation behind those in widespread service in the West. Foremost, just like the MiG-23, the MiG-25P was optimised for high-speed interceptor operations and required the full support of the PVO's highly-integrated air defence network: for this purpose, both types were equipped with the Lasour datalink, which – at least in the USSR – worked in conjunction with the highly-automated Vozdukh-1 computer-supported system that integrated the work of manned interceptors with that of the SAMs. With the help of the Vozdukh-1 and the Lasour, the commander on the ground could simultaneously vector dozens of interceptors automatically or semi-automatically onto their targets, along an optimum flight path and without any kind of voice communication.[3]

FULCRUM

Finally realising that the MiG-23 would be at a great disadvantage if failing to destroy enemy fighters in a first attack with its R-23s, in the early 1970s the GenStab went a step further and ordered the development of an entirely new, agile tactical fighter-interceptor, which was to lack nothing in manoeuvring performance. Once again, development took time and although first-flown in October 1977, the resulting MiG-29 initially suffered from unreliable engines as much as from poor avionics. The result was a number of compromises, including the widespread use of what would be considered 'obsolete' technologies in the West. The centrepiece of the MiG-29's weapon system became the N019 Rubin (ASCC/NATO-codename Slotback) look-down/shoot-down radar, coupled with the OEPS-29 KOLS IRST and a laser rangefinder. In the 'head-on mode' (similar to the AWG-9's TWS), the N019 could track up to 10 targets out to a range of 80km (43nm) simultaneously. Standard armament consisted of two brand-new R-27 medium-range missiles (ASCC/NATO-codename AA-10 Alamo) with a

The MiG-25PD of the PVO. This version came into being in 1976 in reaction to Belenko's defection to Japan. It was equipped with a more powerful version of the MiG-23ML's radar, but never exported in that configuration. On the contrary, the MiG-25PD/PDS export version retained the – slightly modified – Smerch-A2 radar. (US DoD)

maximum theoretic range of 58km (31nm), and four R-60 short-range missiles. Entering service in the USSR only in 1984, the MiG-29 was offered for export just two years later: customers outside the WTO received the sub-variant designated 9.12B, which featured a modified N019EB radar (with fewer working modes than the variant operated by the VVS), and a different IFF.[4]

TABLE 3: SOVIET AIR-TO-AIR MISSILES ENCOUNTERED IN COMBAT BY USN TOMCATS, 1987-1999

SOVIET DESIGNATION	ASCCN/NATO	NOTES
R-3S	AA-2A Atoll	IR-homing
R-13M	AA-2D Atoll	IR-homing, minimal front-aspect capability
R-40R	AA-6A Acrid-A	SARH
R-40T	AA-6B Acrid-B	IR-homing
R-40RD	AA-6C Acrid-C	SARH
R-40TD	AA-6D Acrid-D	IR-homing
R-23R	AA-7A Apex-A	SARH
R-23T	AA-7B Apex-B	IR-homing
R-27R	AA-10A Alamo-A	SARH
R-60K	AA-8 Aphid	the same ASCC/NATO designation was used for all R-60 variants, including the R-60K and R-60MK

3
PHANTOMS OF IRAN

As mentioned in Chapter 1, Iran became not only the sole export customer for the F-14, but its order for 80 Tomcats then saved the entire project. Ironically, the first air-to-air action involving Tomcats of the US Navy in the Middle East pitted them against fighter jets of the Iranian air force – not against Iranian F-14s, but an older model originally developed for the Navy.

IRAN-IRAQ WAR

On 22 September 1980, Iraq invaded Iran. Unknown to either of the sides involved, what was initially expected to be a short war by almost everybody involved, eventually became one of the longest, biggest, and most merciless conventional armed conflicts of the 20th century, constantly fuelled by all sorts of age-old rivalries of ethnic and religious origins, and meddling by foreign powers. The Iraqis initiated their onslaught at an opportune moment: the US ally Shah Mohammed Reza Pahlavi II of Iran was toppled by months-long mass demonstrations against his rule and his alliance with Washington. Iran then plunged into an outright civil war won by the Shi'a clergy intolerant of anything even distantly connected to the 'Great Satan' – the USA. Equipped and trained by the Americans, the Iranian armed forces found themselves exposed to a series of purges, including the liquidation of all top commanders, and the arrest and detention, or forced retirement of nearly 50% of mid-ranking officers. By 1980, the Army was essentially demobilised and the air force grounded.[1]

However, once the Iraqis invaded, the Iranians scrambled to recover what was left of their military might: with their army still in

An elevated bow view of USS *Constellation* (CV-64) with aircraft of CVW-14 on deck: Tomcats of VF-21 and VF-154 can be seen parked at the stern.

chaos, it was up to the air force – re-named to the Islamic Republic of Iran Air Force (IRIAF) – to carry the burden of the battle. Theoretically, the IRIAF was in a good position to do so: as well as 80 F-14As acquired between 1973 and 1978 (79 of which were delivered), since 1966, Iran had bought not only 105 Northrop F-5A and 23 F-5Bs, 15 RF-5As, 32 F-4Ds, 177 F-4Es, 16 RF-4Es, and 166 Northrop F-5E/Fs, but also the entire infrastructure necessary to maintain and operate the aircraft and most of their avionics and weaponry. While many F-5A/Bs were returned to the USA in the mid-1970s, and some other jets were written off during routine training operations, the mass of F-4D/Es, F-5E/Fs and F-14s were still around, as were most of their pilots. Fighting with all means available, they fought the Iraqi invasion of south-western Iran to a standstill in the Battle of Khuzestan in October and November 1980.

TABLE 4: CVW-14, WEST PACIFIC & INDIAN OCEAN CRUISE, 1987		
SQUADRON	AIRCRAFT TYPE	MODEX
VF-154 Black Knights	F-14A	NK1xx
VF-21 Freelancers	F-14A	NK2xx
VFA-113 Stingers	F/A-18A	NK3xx
VFA-25 Fist of the Fleet	F/A-18A	NK4xx
VA-196 Main Battery	A-6E/KA-6D	NK5xx
VAW-113 Black Hawks	E-2C	NK6xx
VAQ-139 Cougars	EA-6B	NK6xx
HS-8 Eightballers	SH-3H	NK6xx
VS-37 Sawbucks	S-3A	NK7xx

OPERATION EARNEST WILL

Simultaneously with the Battle of Khuzestan, the IRIAF ran such a highly-effective offensive against its enemy's oil industry, that Iraq ceased to export crude and gas; indeed, Baghdad was forced to import fuels and did not manage to reach its pre-war oil exports even as of 1990, two years after the Iran-Iraq War ended. De-facto bankrupt by 1981, Iraq depended on extensive financial support from Kuwait, Saudi Arabia, and the United Arab Emirates to retain the ability to continue the war against Iran. Unsurprisingly, the Iraqis sought to knock out the Iranian oil industry but lacked the necessary firepower and reach. When all other attempts failed, in 1984 they began attacking tankers exporting Iranian crude from Khark Island in the northern Persian Gulf, thus initiating what became known as the 'Tanker War'. With this campaign being micromanaged by a government in Baghdad that had no understanding for modern armed forces, it degenerated into a battle of attrition: despite occasional successes, it proved costly while failing to stop Iranian oil exports. However, it proved volatile enough to provoke Tehran into a short-sighted decision to order its forces into intercepting foreign merchants underway to countries supporting Iraq in the Persian Gulf, including Kuwait, which slowly crystallised as the second most important US ally in the area. Related Iranian activities offended the Kuwaitis and incensed them to a degree where they requested help from Washington: if the USA were not to bow, they threatened to ask the Soviets instead. The administration of US President Ronald Reagan rushed to agree and 12 Kuwaiti supertankers were re-registered to

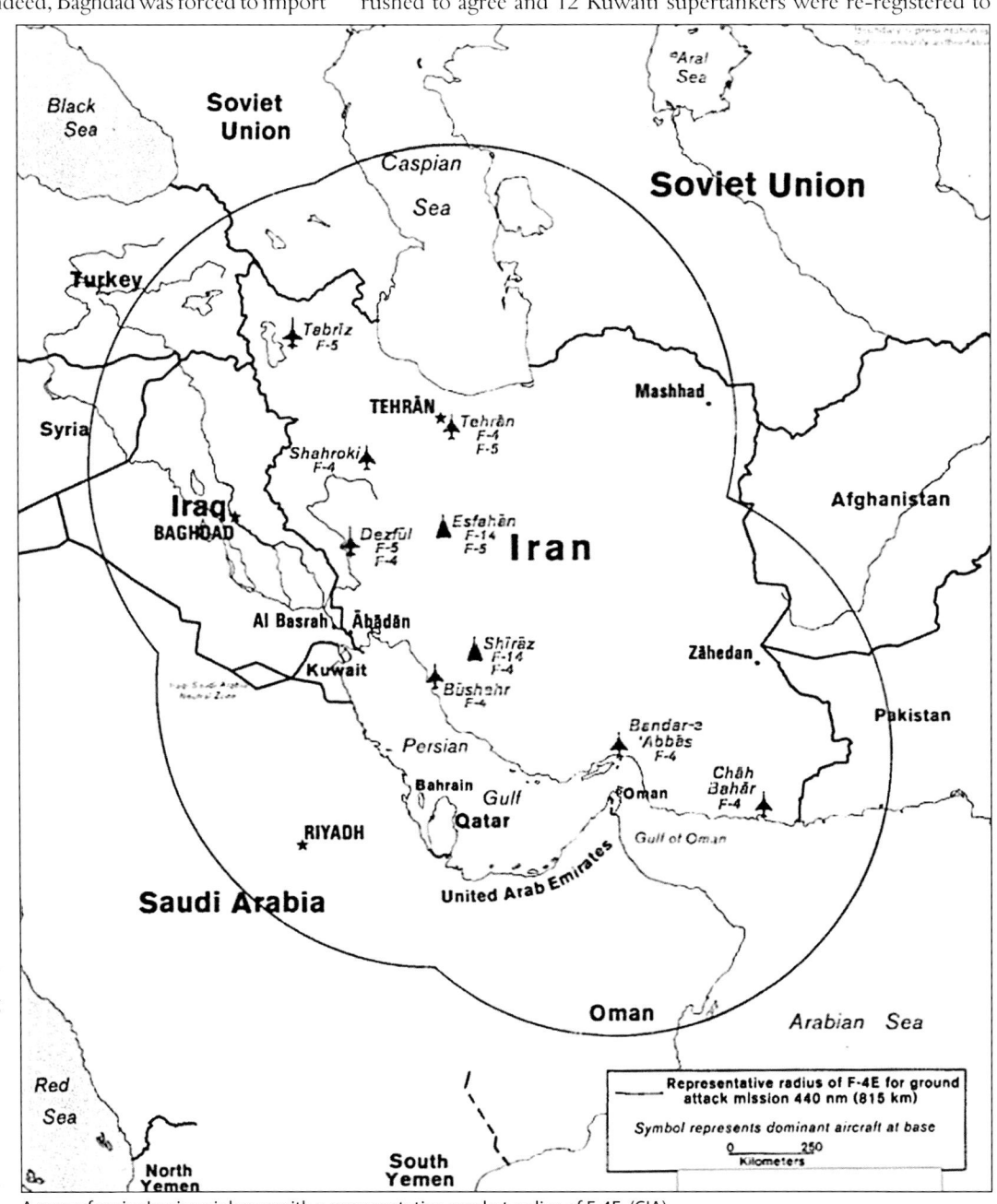

A map of major Iranian air bases with a representative combat radius of F-4E. (CIA)

This AIM-7E-2 Sparrow and AIM-9J Sidewinder-armed F-4E was photographed in the 1990s while operated by the Bushehr-based 61st TFS. It wore the same camouflage pattern as the F-4Es of the 91st TFS and is seen here over similar terrain to that in the Bandar-e Abbas area. (Tom Cooper Collection)

the USA: in the future, these were to pass up and down the Persian Gulf escorted by USN warships in Operation Earnest Will. After months of preparations, in July 1987 the Navy concentrated a CVBG of nearly a dozen warships, centred on USS *Constellation* at the so-called Gonzo Station in the Gulf of Oman. Underway with CVW-14 aboard (see Table 4 for details), the carrier was not to enter the Persian Gulf, but to provide top cover from there. The ships heading into the Gulf were to be protected by two Lockheed P-3C Orion maritime patrol aircraft, forward deployed at Dhahran in Saudi Arabia. While packed full of advanced radars and electronic gear, these aircraft depended on the protection of F-14s.

TEHRAN'S MASTER PLAN

The widely publicised concentration of USN warships sounded alarm bells in Tehran. Ever since the failed attempt, in April 1980, to rescue hostages held by the Iranian revolutionaries in the US embassy in Tehran, the Iranian government was aware that the Navy's carriers were 'somewhere nearby' and capable of launching strikes at it. Moreover, the clergy-dominated government in Tehran suspected Washington – often with good reasons – for not only supporting Baghdad's war effort, but for outright cooperation: such suspicions were further increased once Iranian military intelligence was informed about the arrival of the US military liaison mission to the Iraqi capital. From the Iranian point of view, this meant that the Americans were now directly involved in the ongoing Iran-Iraq War and providing direct support for Baghdad. The Iranian military commanders were fully aware that their forces could not confront the USN and for good reason: most were trained in the USA, and their troops and aircraft were busy fighting the Iraqis. By July 1987, the IRIAF was down to about 100 fully mission capable aircraft and a similar number of pilots, exhausted by years of intensive fighting. Nevertheless, the 'hawks' in Tehran won the day and the Iranian armed forces received the order to challenge the Americans in asymmetric fashion: the naval service of the Islamic Revolutionary Guard Corps (IRGC) was to do so by deploying mines, while the IRIAF would act by trying to sneak up on one of the US aircraft the Iranians understood were supporting Iraqi anti-ship operations along their coast of the Persian Gulf. That said, a direct confrontation was to be avoided at any cost, unless there was a suitable opportunity to 'teach arrogant Americans a lesson'.[2]

MINES OFF FARSI

The first USN convoys for Kuwait set sail from the port of Fujairah in the Gulf of Oman on 22 July 1987. There was lots of excitement on the US side, especially when the ships – including supertankers SS *Bridgetown* and SS *Gas Prince*, escorted by the guided missile cruiser USS *Fox* (CG-33), guided missile destroyer USS *Kidd* (DDG-993), and guided missile frigate USS *Cromelin* (FFG-37) – entered Hormuz during the first leg of their voyage. Passing the strait by night, the two re-flagged tankers and three escorting warships experienced no incidents. It was only on the morning of 23 July 1987, that two F-4Es from the 91st TFS attempted to take a look: both distanced as soon as being warned not to approach any closer, still about 24km (15nm) away. Then, about 24 hours later, the re-flagged tanker SS *Bridgetown* hit a mine while passing Farsi Island in the central Persian Gulf. Although causing relatively minor damage to this 'ultra-large crude carrier' this incident was a huge embarrassment for the proud US Navy. Meanwhile it had more than 20 warships and 90 aircraft in the Persian Gulf and the Gulf of Oman, yet failed to protect the convoy because none of these assets could cope with mines. Moreover, while this convoy was underway, an Iranian warship intercepted and attacked the Kuwaiti tanker SS *Jebel Ali*, which enjoyed no US protection. The big question was: what would happen next?

SHARKS OF BANDAR-E-ABBAS

The main Iranian military installation in the lower Persian Gulf – indeed: in the centre of the Hormuz Straits – was Tactical Fighter Base 9 (TFB.9). Constructed in 1975-1976 outside Bandar-e Abbas, it housed the last 36 F-4Es delivered to Iran. Originally, these were planned to be operated by two units: the 91st Tactical Fighter Squadron (TFS) – nicknamed the 'Sharks of Bandar-e Abbas' – was established in 1977. However, the second unit was never officially commissioned. During the war with Iraq, the mass of these F-4Es, their spares, weaponry, and their crews, were redeployed to bases further north-west, to replace combat attrition. As of July 1987, the 91st TFS was down to only two F-4Es in operational condition, and only one with a fully mission capable weapon system: the Phantom in question was armed with two AIM-7E-2 Sparrow and two AIM-9J-1 Sidewinder air-to-air missiles and kept on quick reaction alert (QRA). These were the same two F-4s encountered by USN warships on 24 July 1987. The other asset worth mentioning at Bandar-e Abbas at the time was the nearby radar station equipped with a Westinghouse APS-4 long-range early warning system: completed in 1978, this proved capable of detecting a MiG-21-sized target from a range of more than 250 kilometres (135nm). This radar station was to play a crucial role in the sole Iranian attempt to challenge the US aircraft involved in Operation Earnest Will, and thus the first of the actual stories of this book.

AIR BATTLE IN THE SOUP

Early on the morning of 8 August 1987, the APS-4 at Bandar-e Abbas detected a target moving slowly towards the northern entrance of the Hormuz Strait. From tracking a similar movement over the previous weeks, the Iranians figured out that the aircraft in question was one of the USN's P-3Cs. Considering it appeared to be alone, it was a 'perfect target': a slow and nearly defenceless target, suspected of collecting intelligence about the movement of shipping up and down the Iranian coast, and forwarding the same to Baghdad. Minutes later, one F-4E of the 91st TFS was ordered into the air. Once airborne, Major Darious Kaknegar Moghadam with Captain Mahdi Shaghayegh as weapons system officer (WSO), flew along the coast towards the west, at an altitude of about 213m (700ft). Keeping their APQ-120 radar on standby, Kaknegar and Shaghayegh waited for a signal from the ground control to execute the planned pop-up manoeuvre and attack.[3]

Major Darious Kaknegar Moghadam, the pilot from the 91st TFS, IRIAF that engaged a P-3C Orion of the USN with a single AIM-7E-2 Sparrow on 8 August 1987. (via Tom Cooper)

However, the weather in the Persian Gulf that day was very hot and humid, with dense overcast from 300 up to about 7,000 metres (984-22,966ft). The clouds – and the sand these contained – played havoc with radars on both sides. For a start, even the excellent APS-4 system missed the appearance of two Tomcats from VF-21 on a CAP at an altitude of 6,100m (20,000ft) over the Hormuz. The leader of the USN formation was Lieutenant-Commander (LCDR) Robert Clement, CO VF-21; on his wing was Lieutenant (LT) William 'Bear' Ferran, a young pilot on his first operational cruise. The two Tomcats were supported by an E-2C Hawkeye from VAW-113 Black Hawks.

The Hawkeye detected the Phantom right after its take-off from Bandar-e Abbas and monitored its progress in a western direction. Because it flew in the rough direction of the Orion, several warnings were aired: usually, the Iranians would react by turning away. Not this time: Kaknegar headed straight for his slow target. Therefore, the E-2C ordered the P-3C in a southern direction, and Clement and Ferran to engage. With Ferran's AWG-9 having a better track, he took the lead and both Tomcats engaged their afterburners, accelerating towards two targets now 65km (35nm) away. Kaknegar continued and, on advice from ground control, initiated a shallow climb to 610m (2,000ft). When within

Captain Mahdi Shaghayegh, Kaknegar's RIO for the missions on 24 July and 8 August 1987, seen after the war in front of one of the F-4Ds of the 101st TFS, IRIAF. (Mahdi Mehmandoost Collection)

F-14A BuNo 161607, Modex NK202, was the Tomcat crewed by LT William 'Bear' Ferran during the clash with two IRIAF F-4Es on 8 August 1987. Two Sparrows were fired from the jet: one malfunctioned but the other peppered the Phantom's fin with shrapnel.

20km (11nm) of the Orion, the Iranian powered up his APQ-120, Shaghayegh quickly locked on the Orion: the pilot waited for three seconds to permit the system to set up all parameters, then squeezed the trigger. Another two seconds later, his AIM-7E-2 Sparrow thundered away, dropping a bit before climbing up and to the front of the F-4E, releasing a typical trail of white smoke.

The fact that the Iranians had powered up their radar and locked-on to the P-3C did not escape the attention of the Americans. On the contrary, it made the situation clear. Now it was a matter of urgency to stop the Iranian attack. Ferran's RIO quickly set up his counterattack and, at a range of 16km (8.6nm) the pilot fired one AIM-7F. The missile dropped from the Tomcat like a stone: its motor failed to ignite. Realising what was going on, Clement followed up with an AIM-7M and fired 'from well inside 15 kilometres (7.5nm)'. Ferran then fired another AIM-7F. Both of these Sparrows were released in a mad rush and from the verge of their envelope, at a target neither American could see: the hope of a hit was minimal, but still there. The hope of Kaknegar and Shaghayegh was much higher: they could not see their target either, but the smoke trail of their missile was indicative of the weapon guiding and they were expecting it to hit at any time. Then, all of a sudden, their RWR blared a warning: a quick look at the display indicated an airborne threat and that their aircraft had been fired upon. Acting instinctively, Kaknegar forgot about his Sparrow, broke hard and dived for the sea surface, invisible in the soup of clouds and dust below him.

Ferran was strained while following the two smoke trails down: he saw his Sparrow drifting slightly from left to right and then, shortly after motor burn-out, he noticed a fireball inside the translucent diamond projected on his HUD, marking target's position. At least at the time, Clement was certain *his* missile scored a kill. Kaknegar never looked back: his peripheral vision registered 'something' flashing past his cockpit before detonating 'somewhere behind': actually only metres behind his Phantom. Taking no chances, he concentrated on his altimeter to roll out above the shark-infested waters, then thundered away towards the north, accelerating to supersonic speed despite the damaged fin. Meanwhile, unable to see any kind of wreckage and thus uncertain what he had engaged, Clement ordered a hard break: leaving a trail of chaff and flares in their wake, both Tomcats dived for the sea surface and disengaged towards the west before ever seeing their target.

The fin of Kaknegar and Shaghayegh's F-4E seen on return from their mission on 8 August 1987, showing the damage caused by one of two Sparrows that detonated near the port horizontal stabiliser. (Tom Cooper Collection)

UNPLEASANT EXPERIENCE

Although no fewer than four Sparrows (of three different versions!) were fired in this engagement, none scored a hit: one failed on launch, another proximity fused a few metres behind the target, and two missed because the launching aircraft turned away, breaking the radar lock-on in the process. Considering LCDR Clement stopped guiding his AIM-7M before the hit, while LT Ferran observed a detonation of his second Sparrow, it is apparent that – while not a 'hard kill' – the latter pilot scored a 'soft kill', thus spoiling Kaknegar and Shaghayeghs's attack through forcing them to evade, and saving the lives of those aboard of the targeted P-3C.[4]

Ironically, the experience of the USN pilots involved were not entirely pleasant. Due to the weather, their superiors were uncertain if there were any IRIAF Phantoms around at all: while commended by some for successfully protecting the so-called 'high-value unit' (HVU), Ferran was criticised for opening fire at a 'fake radar echo', supposedly created by bad weather; and by others for mishandling his weapon system and firing Sparrows 'wildly'. Before long, the damage was done: while subsequently sent to the coveted Naval Fighter Weapons school (NWFS, better known as 'Topgun'), he eventually left the service in disgust.

4
KUWAIT CRISIS

Only months after the end of the Iran-Iraq War in August 1988, the government in Baghdad began searching for a new object for its animosities. Following a short period of tensions with Syria in 1989, Baghdad began developing plans for a war with Israel in early

USS *Independence* was the first of the Navy's aircraft carriers to reach the crisis zone in reaction to the Iraqi invasion of Kuwait. The carrier passed the Hormuz Strait on 5 August. On the same day, F-14As of VF-21 and VF-154 (pictured) began flying combat air patrols (CAPs) over the northern Persian Gulf.

TABLE 5: USN AIR WINGS OF OPERATION DESERT STORM, 1991

UNIT	AIRCRAFT	AIRCRAFT CARRIER
CVW-1 (AB)		**USS America (CV-66)**
VF-102 Diamondbacks	F-14A/TARPS	AB100
VF-33 Starfighters	F-14A	AB200
VFA-82 Marauders	F/A-18C	AB300
VFA-86 Sidewinders	F/A-18C	AB400
VA-85 Buckeyes	A-6E/KA-6D	AB500
VAW-123 Screwtops	E-2C	AB600
VAQ-137 Rooks	EA-6B	AB620
VS-32 Maulers	S-3B	AB700
HS-11 Dragonslayers	SH-3H	
CVW-2 (NE)		**USS Ranger (CV-61)**
VF-1 Wolfpack	F-14A	NE100
VF-2 Bounty Hunters	F-14A/TARPS	NE200
VA-145 Swordsmen	A-6E/KA-6D	NE300
VA-155 Silver Foxes	A-6E/KA-6D	NE400
VAW-116 Sun Kings	E-2C	NE600
VAQ-131 Lancers	EA-6B	NE620
VS-38 Red Griffins	S-3A	NE700
HS-14 Chargers	SH-3H	
CVW-3 (AC)		**USS John F Kennedy (CV-67)**
VF-14 Tophatters	F-14A	AC100
VF-32 Swordsmen	F-14A/TARPS	AC200
VA-46 Clansmen	A-7E	AC300
VA-72	A-7E	AC400
VA-75 Sunday Punchers	A-6E/KA-6D	AC500
VAW-136 Seahawks	E-2C	AC600
VAQ-130 Zappers	EA-6B	AC620
VS-22 Vidars	S-3B	AC700
HS-7 Big Dippers	SH-3H	
CVW-5 (NF)		**USS Midway (CV-41)**
VFA-195 Dam Busters	F/A-18A	NF100
VFA-151 Vigilantes	F/A-18A	NF200
VFA-192 Golden Dragons	F/A-18A	NF300
VA-185 Nighthawks	A-6E	NF400
VA-115 Eagles	A-6E/KA-6D	NF500
VAW-115 Sentinels	E-2C	NF600
VAQ-136 Gauntlets	EA-6B	NF620
HS-12 Wyverns	SH-3H	
CVW-8 (AJ)		**USS Theodore Roosevelt (CVN-71)**
VF-41 Black Aces	F-14A	AJ100
VF-84 Jolly Rogers	F-14A/TARPS	AJ200
VFA-15 Vallions	F/A-18C	AJ300
VFA-87 Golden Warriors	F/A-18C	AJ400
VA-65 Tigers	A-6E	AJ500
VA-36 Roadrunners	A-6E/KA-6D	AJ530
VAW-124 Bear Aces	E-2C	AJ600
VAQ-141 Shadowhawks	EA-6B	AJ620
VS-24 Scouts	S-3B	AJ700
HS-9 Sea Griffins	SH-3H	
CVW-17 (AA)		**USS Saratoga (CV-60)**
VF-74 Bedevilers	F-14A+	AA100
VF-103 Sluggers	F-14A+/TARPS	AA200
VFA-83 Rampagers	F/A-18C	AA300
VFA-81 Sunliners	F/A-18C	AA400
VA-35 Black Panthers	A-6E/KA-6D	AA500
VAW-125 Tigertails	E-2C	AA600
VAQ-132 Scorpions	EA-6B	AA620
VS-30 Diamondcutters	S-3B	AA700
HS-3 Tridents	SH-3H	

1990. To 'clear the deck' for such a massive conflict, it first had to free itself of the massive foreign debt accumulated during the eight years of fighting Iran. Saudi Arabia and the United Arab Emirates agreed relatively quickly to write off Iraqi debts, but Kuwait – a state that Iraqi nationalists had claimed sovereignty over for decades – refused to do so. When related negotiations failed, on 2 August 1990 Iraq invaded and, after less than 48 hours of fighting, occupied the country.[1]

The Iraqi invasion and subsequent unilateral accession of Kuwait drew massive international condemnation: the United Nations imposed an arms embargo upon Baghdad and demanded an unconditional withdrawal. Moreover, the government of Saudi Arabia, and the exiled government of Kuwait requested military aid from the USA and other allies in the West and elsewhere. As a consequence, huge military contingents from more than 20 nations were rushed to the Persian Gulf in the operation code-named Desert Shield. When negotiations failed, the United States – in agreement with the United Nations – issued an ultimatum for Iraqi forces to be withdrawn from Kuwait by 15 January 1991. When Baghdad showed no intentions to bow, it was obvious that there would be a war.

DEPLOYMENT

Units of the US Navy were some of the first to receive the order to deploy to the Persian Gulf in reaction to the Iraqi invasion of Kuwait. Re-routed in this direction on 3 August 1990, the CVBG centred on the aircraft carrier USS *Independence* (CV-62) entered the Persian Gulf only two days later. Embarked aircraft of CVW-14, including F-14As from VF-21 and VF-154, were initially deployed to fly combat air patrols (CAPs) off the coast of Saudi Arabia, and thus protect vital ports and other installations necessary for the deployment of US and allied forces. On 8 August 1990, USS *Dwight D Eisenhower* (CVN-69), with CVW-7 aboard (including F-14As from VF-142 and VF-143), passed the Suez Canal and took a station in the northern Red Sea, from where it was able to bolster air defences of northern Saudi Arabia. Two further CVBGs – centred on USS *Saratoga* (CV-60, with CVW-17 aboard) and USS *John F Kennedy* (CV-67, with CVW-3 aboard) – were to follow by mid-September

A DANGEROUS LEFT-OVER

At the high point of the 'Tanker War', in late 1986, the Iraqis had a Dassault Falcon 50, operated on behalf of their General Military Intelligence Directorate (GMID), flown to Villaroche in France, where it was subjected to an unusual conversion. The jet received the weapons system of the Mirage F.1EQ-5 fighter-bomber – including the Cyrano IVQ-C5 radar and two hardpoints for AM.39 Exocet anti-ship missiles. Back in Iraq in February 1987, it was subjected to a series of comprehensive tests before it was deployed in combat for the first – and only – time. On the evening of 17 May 1987, it was flown down the Saudi side of the Persian Gulf, before turning east, and releasing two Exocets: both struck the guided missile frigate USS *Stark*, killing 37 of her crew.

Code-named *Suzanna* (probably after the French girlfriend of one of the Iraqis involved), the Falcon 50 in question was never deployed in combat again. However, and although officials in Washington made repeated statements that the attack on the USS *Stark* was flown by an 'Iraqi Mirage', henceforth, the ONI was on alert and 'very aware' of the jet's existence and capabilities. *Suzanna* caused serious concerns that the Iraqis might deploy it via Jordan and into the northern Red Sea, and attack one of the US Navy's warships there: the threat that the modified business jet emanated was constantly on the minds of everybody embarked aboard the CVBGs operating in the Red Sea. It was for this reason that ever since the first USN CVBGs arrived on station in that area, in August 1990, its Tomcats flew rigorous CAPs above the carriers, 24/7, and aggressively intercepted whatever came their way. The patrols in question were continued all through operations Desert Shield and Desert Storm, from August 1990 until March 1991, and – regardless of so many other urgencies – the USAF supported them by providing at least one KC-135 around the clock.

How tense such CAPs could get became clear in August 1990, when one of the Aegis cruisers deployed in the northern Red Sea detected a high-speed aircraft approaching from the north, and a pair of Tomcats kept on alert was scrambled to inspect. By accident, David 'Hey Joe' Parsons, a RIO serving with the VF-32, was in the rear cockpit of one of two F-14As returning from a training sortie over Saudi Arabia:

> Our mission that day took us into Saudi Arabia and out of the Kennedy's control. However, as we switched back into the Red Sea control frequency, we could hear excited dialogue about a high-speed flying and alert aircraft being launched and ships going on general quarters. We were well to the north-east of the ships and, from what I could tell, in the best position to execute an intercept. Thus, I checked in [and] advised the controller that we were ready, willing and able to do so.
>
> The TAO's voice was several octaves higher than normal and they were going into "warning red, weapons tight". As we swung our nose in the direction of the vector we got, I got an immediate lock on an extremely fast and high-flying aircraft. The TCS could not resolve the identification, but I had a 300mm camera lens in my bag and broke it out. The AWG-9 was giving us a huge lead via the steering cue, so I was looking out the starboard side – as we spotted a white contrail high above us. As I twisted the lens, the beautiful silhouette of the Concorde came into focus…

Identified as a supersonic airliner, the jet was left to continue its voyage. After the end of the Second Persian Gulf War it became known that the Iraqis had evacuated *Suzanna* to Iran in late January 1991 – but without her weapons system: ever since, the jet has been used for VIP-transport in Iran.

A photograph showing the Falcon 50 registered as YI-ALE before the addition of the weapons system of the Mirage F.1EQ-5. (Ahmad Sadik Collection, via Tom Cooper)

Aérospatiale-BAC Concorde, the only supersonic passenger aircraft to ever enter regular service, caught by the 300mm zoom of David Parson's camera during the interception high above the Red Sea in August 1990. (Photo by CDR David Parsons, USN, ret.)

A poor quality but highly interesting still from a video showing the pointy end of 'Suzanna' as of 1990: this covered the Cyrano IVQ-C5 radar. The jet included not only the weapons system of the Mirage F.1EQ-5 but had the full instrumentation of that type installed in the right side of its cockpit. By 1990, it was further modified through the addition of an extra fuel tank inside the cabin, and the capability to carry either a Raphael-TH pod with SLAR (visible under the fuselage) or an RP.35 drop tank with capacity of 1,500 litres of fuel. (via Tom Cooper)

1990. With this, the Navy had no fewer than three carriers in the Red Sea and one in the Persian Gulf. While sufficient to defend the Saudi desert kingdom, this was still considered insufficient for the task of liberating Kuwait. Moreover, *Independence* and *Eisenhower* had to be relieved on station. Correspondingly, in November 1990, four additional CVBGs were ordered to the Middle East. These were centred on carriers USS *Midway* (CV-41), with CVW-5 aboard, which included no F-14s; USS *Ranger* (CV-61), with CVW-2 (VF-1 and VF-2); USS *America*, with CVW-1 (VF-102 and VF-33); and USS *Theodore Roosevelt* (CVN-71), with CVW-8 (VF-41 and VF-84). The last three of these reached the area only in mid-January 1991, by when *Independence* and *Eisenhower* were withdrawn. The US Navy's embarked aviation thus went into Operation Desert Storm – an enterprise aimed to destroy the Iraqi war-fighting capability and then liberate Kuwait, initiated in early hours of 16 January 1991 – with units as listed in Table 5.

ORGANISATION OF THE BATTLEFIELD

Of course, the USN was not alone in running its build-up in the Middle East in late 1990. On the contrary, a total of more than 2,000 combat and support aircraft, over 150 warships, over 500,000 troops, 3,000 armoured vehicles and 2.2 million tonnes of armament, vehicles, ammunition and supplies from more than 30 countries were rushed to Saudi Arabia and neighbouring countries during Operation Desert Shield. Unsurprisingly, this resulted in an incredibly complex command structure. Ultimately, although not in control over all the Arab and allied forces, the US Central Forces Command (CENTCOM) became the arbiter and deviser of the grand strategy, and the command node responsible for fighting Iraq and liberating Kuwait. With the US Air Force deploying the largest and best equipped flying component subjected to CENTCOM's command, it was up to its in-theatre commander, Lieutenant-General Charles Horner, and his Special Planning Group to outline an offensive air campaign. Of course, this planning cell – formalised as the Combined Air Operations Centre (CAOC) and the Joint Targeting Coordination Board (JTCB) – included representatives of the USN and other involved air forces. However, this made the work of both instances extremely complex. On one hand, they had to organise and run a coherent operation, regardless of controlling very disparate forces, the commanders of which – and also those of the United States Naval Forces Central Command (NAVCENT) – all had their own priorities. On the other hand, for security-related reasons, it could only share full details about its decision-making processes with a very limited number of officers. With there being no doubt that it was the USAF that was 'running the show', a natural result was that many myths emerged about the way 'USAF people' were arriving at their decisions.

RULES OF ENGAGEMENT

While the USN already favoured the development of fast interceptors armed with radar-guided missiles capable of engaging beyond visual range (BVR) during the second half of the 1950s, resulting in the development of the F-4 Phantom II, experience from local conflicts of the 1960s showed that deploying such weapons could easily result

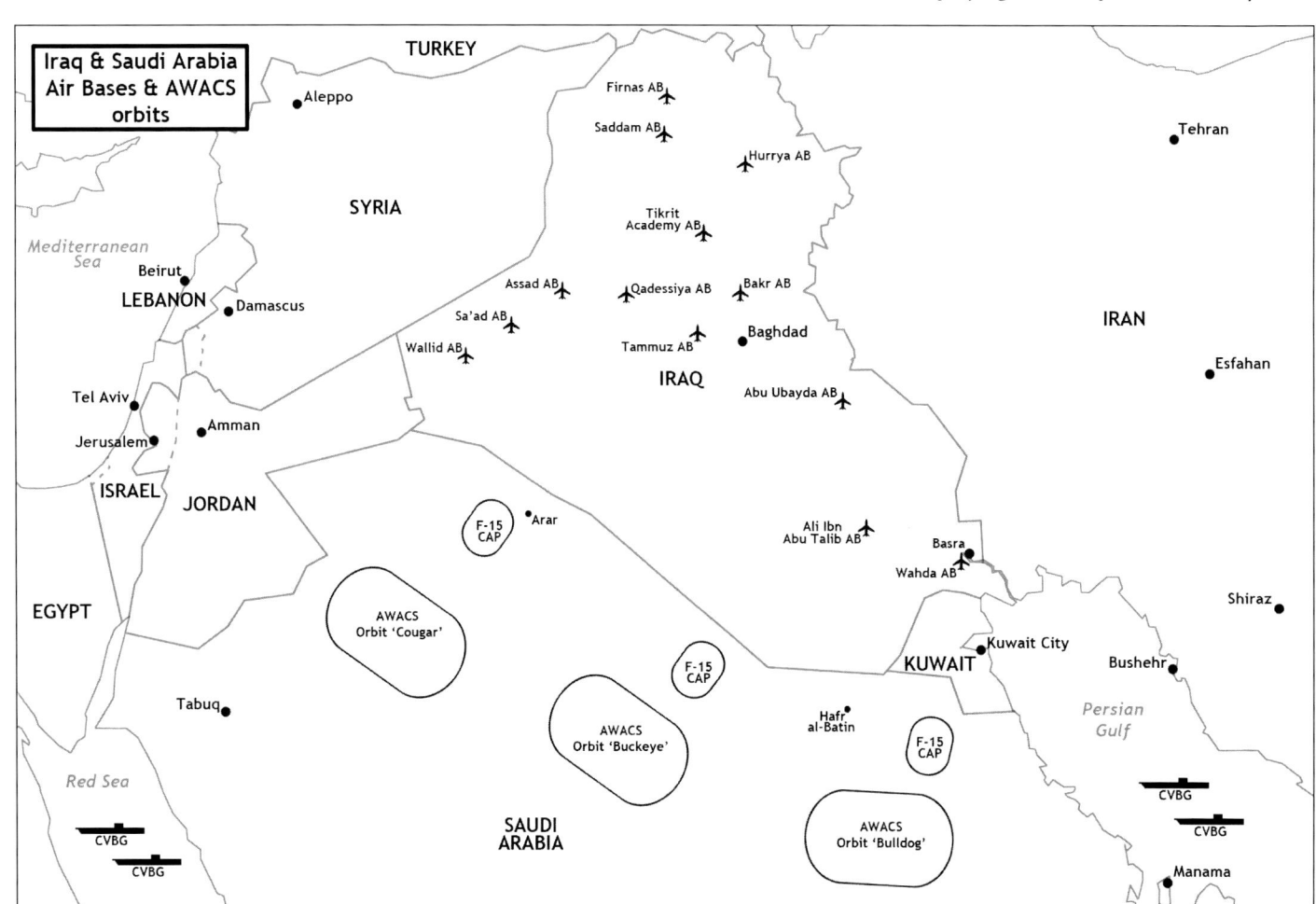

A map showing major IrAF air bases, and the way that the CAOC organised the 'battlefield' over Iraq. The primary tool of command and control for the allied air forces were three 'orbits': patrol stations for Boeing E-3 Sentry AWACS aircraft over northern Saudi Arabia. Thanks to their radar range of about 555km (300nm), and their ESM-systems, AWACS were capable of tracking the work of the Iraqi air defences up to the line connecting Sa'ad AB with Tammuz and Baghdad. (Map by Tom Cooper)

in so-called 'blue-on-blue' incidents: cases where friendly forces were misidentified as enemy, and taken under fire. Indeed, both the Phantoms of the USN and of the USAF had several times opened fire on allied fighter jets, sometimes resulting in painful losses. The consequence was a set of rules of engagement (ROEs) dictating that nobody could open fire without visually identifying the target: with this, the F-4 quickly lost its primary advantage vis-à-vis MiGs operated by the North Vietnamese air force. Some of the BVR capability was recovered only during the last years of that conflict through the development and installation of systems like the AN/APX-80 Combat Tree enemy-IFF-interrogator. This was capable of 'triggering' and 'reading' the (non-decrypted) signals from the Soviet-made SRO-2/Khrom IFF-transponder installed into North Vietnamese MiGs: it enabled their positive identification from dozens of kilometres away, and thus the crews of USAF F-4Ds equipped with it were able to use their AIM-7 Sparrows from beyond visual range. Up to two dozen MiG-kills were scored with help of the 'Tree' in the 1971-1972 period, before the North Vietnamese figured out what the Americans were doing, and limited the use of the SRO-2.[2]

While derivatives of the APX-80 subsequently found widespread use in the USAF, and were even exported to Iran and Israel, due to the acquisition of the expensive F-14, the Navy was so starved of funding that it could not afford the acquisition of similar equipment for its Tomcats. Correspondingly, they received only the AN/APX-76 friendly IFF-interrogator. It was rather on the insistence of F-14 crews that a cheaper solution was found in the form of the AN/AXX-1 Television Camera Set (TCS): this was a camera equipped with a telescopic lens capable of providing a reasonable clear image – and thus visual identification – of big aircraft tracked by the AWG-9 out to a range of about 80km (43nm). The TCS entered service in the early 1980s but was still few in numbers even during engagements with Libya in 1986.

Meanwhile, it was foremost the invention of micro and information technologies that resulted in the emergence of the non-cooperative target recognition (NCTR). Decades previously it was known that radar returns contained more information than the available technology could extract. The solid-state processors enabled this to be rectified and the USAF took care to install the NCTR-software on computers supporting the AN/APG-63 radar of the F-15C, in the form of the MSIP-II upgrade in the early 1980s. The USN installed similar software into the AN/APG-65 radar of the F/A-18 Hornet fighter-bomber in the early 1980s, and intended to follow-up by doing the same with the F-14D, however, none of these were in operational service as of 1990-1991. Moreover, even the NCTR installed into the F-15C was still far from working perfectly. Correspondingly, when planning for the war against Iraq, the CAOC was left without choice but to impose very strict ROEs. These dictated:

- that only crews that had two forms of electronic identification on board were granted autonomous and independent permission to open fire: they did not require talking to anybody before shooting
- if there was only one form of electronic identification available, the crew had to corelate with, and receive permission from, E-2 or E-3 controllers before they could open fire.

No doubt, such ROEs favoured the USAF F-15C crews, because thanks to the installation of the NCTR they could act quicker.

However, this did not mean that the F-14s did not fly fighter sweeps, as widely claimed: they did. Moreover, when underway over Iraq by day, Tomcat crews could still fall back upon their TCS. On its own, this was no major issue: as the subsequent experience was to show, it became one – but because in order to use this system over sufficient range, the AN/AXX-1 had to be slaved to the AWG-9 radar, and the latter had to be working in the PDSTT-mode. For reasons described below (see the 'box' on RWRs), this was guaranteed to alert the enemy pilots.[3]

EXOCET THREAT

For a myriad of reasons, the Iraqi Air Force was essentially unknown in the West in the 1990s: if at all, then it was 'famous' for its above-mentioned assaults on international shipping along the Iranian coast in 1984-1988. The mass of such operations were known to have been undertaken by a custom-tailored variant of the Mirage F.1 fighter-bomber – the F.1EQ-5 – equipped with the Aerospatiale AM.39 Exocet anti-ship missile. This threat was taken extremely seriously by the US Navy because of the Exocets. Concerned that the Iraqis might attempt to repeat the feat by exploiting the 'fog of war' factor and sending their Exocet-armed Mirages to shadow returning fighter-bombers, the NAVCENT set up an additional set of ROEs, including 'delousing' of its and friendly aircraft. Correspondingly, these were to return from attacks on Iraq by flying along only two routes, which were to be carefully monitored

The threat of a sudden Iraqi attack with Exocet anti-ship missiles kept the US Navy on its toes all through operations Desert Shield and then Desert Storm. This photograph shows an F-14A of VF-154 Black Knights in-flight refuelling from a KC-135 tanker of the US Air Force over the Persian Gulf in August 1990.

by F-14s, and two guided missile cruisers equipped with the Aegis air defence system: USS *Bunker Hill* (CG-52) and USS *Mobile Bay* (CG-53). Furthermore, the USN deployed the guided missile cruiser USS *Worden* (CG-18) into a position in the north-eastern Persian Gulf: from that position, the cruiser had a free-fire-zone, and could engage any Iraqi jets attempting to attack ships further south at will. The *Worden* was not to be left on its own, but to be supported by the CAP-station Whiskey-1 – the northernmost such station in the Persian Gulf, occupied since August 1990.[4] That said, the rest of the IrAF was a big unknown, which is why the Defence Intelligence Agency (DIA) and the Office of Naval Intelligence (ONI) spent much of the second half of 1990 collecting and cross-examining firm information about it.

ENEMY INTERCEPTORS

Rather gradually, as more information about the IrAF was collected the emerging intelligence picture became more imposing. Established in 1931, by 1990 the IrAF was a force seasoned in fighting almost two dozen wars and insurgencies, and was organised into about 50 operational squadrons with 620 combat aircraft.[5] Arguably, it lacked so-called 'force multipliers: it did try to obtain AEW/AWACS aircraft through installing French-made Thomson-CSF Tigre-G radars into three Ilyushin Il-76 jet transports, but these proved to lack the necessary performance and none was in operational service. Theoretically more effective, yet next-to-unknown in the West was a modified Boeing 727 airliner, equipped to carry the French-made Thomson-CSF TMV-018 Syrel pods for electronic support measures (ESM), capable of tracking the work of enemy radars and air defence systems, and downloading the collected data to the headquarters in real time with help of a datalink. However, the resulting system, codenamed Faw-727, was of no concern to the USN because it was unlikely that this aircraft would ever get close enough to its warships, and because it could not track the work of combat aircraft. What was of concern was the IrAF fleet of about 100 modern interceptors. As of late 1990, the ONI assessed this as consisting of the following machines:

- 29 MiG-29 (ASCC/NATO-codename Fulcrum)
- 22 MiG-25PD (ASCC/NATO-codename Foxbat-E)
- 22 MiG-23ML (ASCC/NATO-codename Flogger-G)
- 29 Mirage F.1EQ-2/-4/-5
- 5 Mirage F.1EQ-6

In a related assessment the ONI concluded that the MiG-29 was the most serious opponent, while the other types would be of lesser importance: only MiG-29s had overland look-down/shoot-down capability, while MiG-23s and MiG-25s were extremely limited in this discipline, and their equipment suffered from poor reliability.[6]

IRAQI FOXBATS

The Iraqis assessed their interceptor force in an entirely different fashion. From their point of view their most potent interceptors were 19 MiG-25s operated by Nos. 96 and 97 Squadrons. The aircraft in question originally consisted of two batches: the first included 12 aircraft delivered by ship to Basra in summer 1980, all equipped to the same MiG-25P standard as used by the PVO before Belenko's defection to Japan in 1976. Dissatisfied with the old Smerch-A low-PRF radars, the Iraqis flatly refused to accept them: all had to be stored in a hangar at Wahda AB (former RAF Shaiba, outside Basra), pending further negotiations. Although a group of 14 IrAF pilots and a similar number of technicians had meanwhile completed their conversion training in the USSR, the Soviet arms embargo imposed in September 1980 then postponed the process of working-up the fleet and nothing happened until the embargo was lifted in May 1981. Then Moscow – concerned it might lose a good customer due to the French deliveries of Mirage F.1s to Iraq – scrambled to send a team of engineers together with a shipment of RP-25 Smerch-A2 radars (still a low-PRF system with only a depressed-angle capability), Type-26Sh-1 IRSTs, R-40RD, R-40TD, and R-60K missiles. Most of the items in question were developed in the USSR following Belenko's defection to Japan and included improvements designed to reduce the fact that they had been compromised to the Western intelligence: indeed, the Type-26Sh-1 IRST – said to be capable of detecting a fighter-sized target in full afterburner from 25km (13nm) – was an entirely new piece of equipment.[7]

The installation of new equipment resulted in the first 12 Iraqi MiG-25Ps being upgraded to an MiG-25PDS-similar standard. They entered service with No. 97 Squadron in early 1983. Two years later, the Iraqis then acquired a batch of 12 newly-built MiG-25PDs to expand the fleet: as well as carrying their usual armament – which in Iraq next to always consisted of four R-40RD/TDs – these jets had their structure reinforced to carry a giant, 5,000-litre (11,023lb) drop tank, which significantly stretched their effective range. MiG-25PDs were operated by the newly established No. 96 Squadron. During the war with Iran, Iraqi MiG-25 pilots claimed a total of 19 kills against Iranian aircraft, of which one F-4E, one RF-4E, one F-14A, a Fokker F.27 transport, and a Grumman

Photographs of Iraqi MiG-25PD/PDSs taken while these were still operational remain extremely rare. This one shows MiG-25PD (export) serial number 2521 with a group of pilots of No. 96 Squadron inside one of the hardened aircraft shelters at Wallid AB (better known as 'H-3' in the West) in 1988. (via Ali Tobchi)

Gulfstream III bizjet carrying the Algerian Minister of Foreign Affairs (who attempted to negotiate a cease-fire between Baghdad and Tehran), were confirmed independently. In turn, two were claimed as shot down by the Iranians, but the Iraqis denied any such losses. By 1990, the IrAF had 30 pilots for its 19 MiG-25PD/PDSs: however, its operations during the war with Iran were so intensive that there was no time to qualify more than 10 pilots for operations by night and bad weather. Moreover, the high operational costs of this complex type and related maintenance problems meant that only ten MiG-25PD/PDSs were fully mission capable on average, and that each of the two units flying them could usually deploy only a pair of aircraft simultaneously.

IRAQI FULCRUMS

The second most important interceptor in IrAF service as of 1990 was the MiG-29. Originally, Baghdad was expecting a lot from this new type and thus placed an order for 137 between 1986 and 1988. As far as is known, 39 of these had been delivered by August 1990, and they were operated by two units: Nos 6 and 39 Squadrons. However, with the Soviets delivering only R-27R and R-60MK missiles for them – but none of weapons that Western intelligence assessed as the biggest threat, such as the R-27T (IR-homing variant of what the ASCC/NATO codenamed the Alamo) or the R-73E (ASCC/NATO-codename AA-11 Archer) – and due to other weaknesses of its weapon systems, the Iraqis found themselves disappointed by the type and stopped its further acquisition. Indeed, the IrAF became keen to start acquiring the much more powerful Sukhoi Su-27 instead.

Related negotiations were interrupted by the UN-imposed arms embargo of 2 August 1990.[8]

Not to be outdone, once the Kuwait crisis erupted, the IrAF went to some extents to lessen the vulnerability of the MiG-29s' weapon systems through modifying a number of airframes. The most important was the removal of inboard underwing pylons and related stations modified to accept a drop tank (right/starboard side), and a French-made Thompson-CSF TMV-002 Remora self-protection electronic countermeasures (ECM) pod. In turn, the launch rails for R-27R missiles – usually installed on inboard underwing stations – were moved to the centre position. Only the outboard underwing pylons – usually carrying R-60MK IR-homing air-to-air missiles – remained where they used to be. The resulting 'Iraqi Fulcrum' was thus limited to carrying a total of four, instead of the usual six missiles, but was to prove an unpleasant surprise in January 1991.

A particularly useful view of the underside of one of the modified 'Iraqi Fulcrums' (IrAF serial number 29062; construction number 22994) taken after the jet was captured by US Marines in 2003. Notable are 'empty' holders for the inboard underwing hardpoints; launch rails for R-27 missiles that have been moved to the centre underwing position, and the outboard underwing hardpoint (on the left side) with its usual R-60 launch rail. (Tom Cooper Collection)

A semi-profile of one of the modified 'Iraqi Fulcrums' (serial number 29040, construction number 21830) seen after its capture by US troops at the former Tammuz AB in 2006. Notable is that the launch rail for R-27 missiles was moved from its usual inboard underwing position to the central underwing position. (Tom Cooper Collection)

IRAQI FLOGGERS

Theoretically, the largest fleet of advanced interceptors in Iraqi service as of 1990 should have been that of the MiG-23s. Like other export customers outside the WTO, the IrAF was initially refused deliveries of MiG-23Ms: in 1974, it received the much-downgraded MiG-23MS equipped with the entirely unsatisfactory weapons system of the MiG-21S, including the RP-22SM radar with a range of just 20km (10.8nm) and nearly useless R-3S IR-homing air-to-air missiles (ASCC/NATO-code AA-2 Atoll). Permission for export of MiG-23Ms to customers outside Europe was granted only in 1979, when these were almost simultaneously sold to Algeria, Iraq, Libya, and Syria under the designation MiG-23MF: while often described as a 'monkey version', the majority of the aircraft of this variant exported to the Middle East were actually second-hand MiG-23Ms that had served with the PVO and the VVS/FA. Their avionics outfit was so austere because it was originally austere and there was nothing the Soviets could remove from them except the equipment necessary for the deployment of nuclear bombs, and the IFF-system. Moreover, while the first five MiG-23MFs reached Iraq in the summer of 1980, deliveries were stopped when Moscow imposed its arms embargo in September of the same year. Certainly enough, this embargo was lifted in May 1981 – foremost because the Soviets were concerned that they might lose a good customer to France, which meanwhile started deliveries of Mirage F.1EQs (see below for details). However, by then, the damage was done: Iraq went into the war with Iran lacking MiG-23s equipped with medium-range air-to-air missiles, and its MiG-23MSs spent most of the first 12 months of that conflict flying air-to-ground sorties.

The five MiG-23MFs officially entered service with the newly established No. 67 Squadron of the Iraqi Air Force (IrAF) in the summer of 1981 but saw only little operational service before the fleet was complete a year later. The unit claimed its first known kill on 12 July 1982, in the form of an Iranian F-4E reportedly shot down over the Howeyzeh Marshes: while the IRIAF might have lost a Phantom II on this date, no specific details from the Iranian side are available.[9]

One of the reasons for the late export of MiG-23MFs was that around the same time a much more advanced variant became available in the USSR. This was the MiG-23ML, designed not only for high-speed missile attacks, but having its structure reinforced and lightened, and its aerodynamics refined for improved manoeuvrability and the stress of up to 8g in close-in combat. Moreover, it was equipped with the Sapfir-23ML pulse-Doppler radar with a look-down capability and an improved TP-23ML IRST. Its primary armament consisted of two large R-24 air-to-air missiles (which were a further development of the R-23, and thus retained the ASCC/NATO-codename AA-7 Apex). These were available in two variants: the R-24R (SARH) and the R-24T (infra-red homing), each with a maximum engagement range of 27km (25nm). For short-range engagements, MiG-23MLs could be armed with up

A group of pilots from No. 73 Squadron, in front of one of their mounts (MiG-23ML serial number 2566), seen shortly after the end of the war with Iran. Notably, until 1989, IrAF aircraft still wore four-digit serials, applied in the order of their delivery. (via Ali Tobchi)

A still from a video showing an IrAF MiG-23ML modified to carry the French-made Remora ECM-pod (the latter is visible as a grey tube to the left of the front wheel strut). (via Ali Tobchi)

to four R-60 infra-red homing air-to-air missiles (ASCC/NATO-codename 'AA-8 Aphid'): these were highly agile weapons with a maximum range of 8km (4.3nm).[10]

Iraq became the second customer outside the WTO (after Syria) to receive MiG-23MLs, but then became the largest export customer for this variant: in 1982, it placed an order for at least 64 aircraft, and promptly sent a group of hand-picked pilots for conversion training in the USSR. The first 16 MiG-23MLs entered service with a newly established unit, No. 73 Squadron, based at Ali Ibn Abu Talib Air Base (AB), outside Nasiriyah, in July 1984. The second batch entered service with No. 63 Squadron based at al-Bakr AB, a year later. By then, No. 73 Squadron had introduced the new variant to combat in particularly spectacular fashion: on 9 August 1984, two carefully guided MiG-23MLs intercepted a pair of F-14As of the IRIAF over the northern Persian Gulf, and shot down one, killing its pilot – and the leading Iranian air warfare tactician, Colonel Hashem All-e-Agha – using R-60 missiles.

By 1989, the MiG-23ML was the most numerous interceptor in IrAF service. However, only a year later, this was no longer the case. The reason was the same strategic blunder by the government in Baghdad that prompted it into invading Kuwait: when the UN then imposed an arms embargo, about 40% of the Iraqi MiG-23MLs were undergoing overhauls in the USSR and Yugoslavia. Unsurprisingly, none was ever returned to Iraq. Thus, even if Nos 63, 73 and 94 Squadrons, IrAF were not as depleted as assessed by the ONI, the fleet was down to only 35 airframes. On the positive side, an unknown number of remaining MiG-23MLs did receive a significant upgrade – which, apparently, escaped the attention of Western intelligence services: they had their port/left ventral hardpoint for R-60 missiles removed, and a Remora ECM-pod installed instead. While this decreased their warload from four to three air-to-air missiles, it also significantly decreased their vulnerability to early detection and tracking by US-made systems.[11]

As far as is known, there were no engagements between Iraqi MiG-23s and USN F-14s in 1991. However, this is far from confirmed: one reason is that so much detail of IrAF operations during the Second Persian Gulf War remains unknown. Another is that due to the configuration of their intakes and their equipment with the Remora pods, US ESM-systems frequently misidentified Iraqi MiG-23MLs for Mirage F.1EQs. It is thus perfectly possible that some of the engagements mentioned in the next chapter actually involved MiG-23MLs, and not Mirages.

IRAQI MIRAGES

A source of particular pride for the IrAF were four squadrons – Nos. 79, 81, 89, and 91 – equipped with Dassault Mirage F.1EQ fighters and usually assessed (so also by the ONI) as 'operated by the best Iraqi pilots and ground crews'. With their political leadership impressed to the levels of obsession by the Iranian order for the F-14, the Iraqis placed their first order for Mirage F.1s in 1977 – and demanded not only the aircraft, but a technology transfer, including continuous upgrades in regards of avionics and weaponry. Heavily financed by Baghdad's petro-dollars, the French defence sector scrambled to deliver not only the aircraft, but an entire electronic warfare system designed to counter the US and British-made equipment operated by the Iranians. What was originally a simple interceptor equipped with analogue Cyrano-IV low-PRF radar and one obsolete Matra R.530 air-to-air missile was, through the second half of the 1970s and the first half of 1980s converted into a very advanced multi-role fighter. The first variant, F.1EQ, was used only for training of Iraqi personnel in France, and quickly upgraded to the F.1EQ-2 standard before deliveries to Iraq commenced in April 1981: it was equipped with the Cyrano-IVQ radar with an MTI and was made compatible with two each of the brand-new Matra Super 530F SARH and Matra R.550 Magic IR-homing missiles. By 1982, pilots flying it had claimed up to 30 kills against the Iranians (including no fewer than 14 by the deputy CO of No. 79 Squadron): while only some six or seven of these were ever confirmed, these did include three Iranian F-14s. The next variant, the F.1EQ-4, was a custom-tailored fighter-bomber with an advanced navigation system and in-flight refuelling (IFR) capability, while the F.1EQ-5 added not only compatibility with AM.39 Exocets, but also with French-made AS.30L laser-guided missiles. By 1985 the fleet was upgraded through the introduction of Thomson-CSF Sherloc digital radar warning receivers (RWRs), Thompson-CSF TMV-002 Remora and TMV-004 Caiman ECM-pods, Thompson-CSF TMV-018 Syrel ESM-pods and sophisticated Sycomor chaff and flare dispensers. While only six out of 12 examples of the final sub-variant, the F.1EQ-6, were ever delivered to Iraq, they arrived equipped with a Cyrano-IV variant with a limited look-down/shoot-down capability over the sea, additional PO underwing hardpoints for conformal chaff and flare dispensers (replacing Sycomore) and Raphael-TH pods including a side-looking radar (SLAR), capable of downloading the collected intelligence to a network of ground stations in real time. Eventually, the equipment in question enabled the IrAF to deploy its Mirage F.1s to run a year-long campaign against the Iranian oil

The Iraqi fleet of Mirage F.1EQ fighter-bombers and the pilots of the four squadrons operating this type were a matter of great pride in Baghdad – with good reason: advanced equipment like Syrel ESM-pods, visible under the centreline hardpoint of this example, was the core of the IrAF's war-fighting capability. (Ahmed Sadik Collection)

THAT LITTLE RWR THING

The advanced technology installed into the F-14 not only caused the block-obsolescence of many potential adversaries but made aerial warfare a complex issue. The widely-used Soviet-made SPO-3 radar warning receiver (RWR), which entered service in the late 1950s and was installed on all of the MiG-21s and MiG-23s of the 1970s, could not detect emissions of the AWG-9. Combined with the fact that the AIM-54 flew along a ballistic trajectory and attacked its targets from above, the consequence was obvious: during the first years of the war with Iran, many Iraqi pilots never knew they were under attack by an F-14A – until one was hit, or missed by a Phoenix missile.

The situation was only slightly better in the case of the Thompson-CSF TMV-011 BF installed on the Mirage F.1EQ-2/4s: while improved in comparison to the original installed in French aircraft (through the addition of the capability to recognise attacks by US-made radars, as operated by the Iranians), it was an analogue system with a very poor 'display' (essentially consisting of four lamps denoting 'quadrants' around the aircraft) that was often oversaturated by emissions from the AWG-9. Consequently, it tended to show the threat from exactly the opposite direction than was actually the case, thus confusing instead of warning the pilot.

In 1984, Iraq received its first MiG-23MLs equipped with the SPO-10 Sirena-3M RWR: originally developed in the late 1960s, this proved capable of recognising the AWG-9 working in the PDSTT and various pulse modes, but regularly failed to detect emissions in the TWS-mode, resulting in several painful losses. Correspondingly, when adapting French-made Remora ECM-pods to their MiG-23MLs in 1989-1990, the Iraqis took care to also equip these with the SPO-15 Beryoza RWR. In Iraq, this system entered service on MiG-25s in 1983. The SPO-15 had an analogue processor with memory cards, making it capable of recognising a total of about 20 different threats, and then of providing a combination of visual and aural warnings that distinguished whether the enemy radar was working in the search or the track mode. In service, it proved capable of detecting all types of AWG-9 emissions: better yet, the slightly more advanced SPO-15M was linked with chaff dispensers and could automatically trigger these into action.

Exploiting the opportunity, the Iraqis promptly demanded (and paid for) the French to provide a similar RWR for their Mirages. The resulting Thompson-CSF Sherloc was the first digital RWR to enter service with the IrAF, in 1985 – but also one of the most advanced contemporary systems in world-wide service. It not only covered a wide range of frequencies, but included a digital processor with a threat library of 100 modes – including all those of the AWG-9. Meanwhile, the Soviets continued the work on improving the sensitiveness of the SPO-15, resulting in sub-variants capable of detecting AWG-9 emissions from very long ranges. Such were installed into the Iraqi MiG-29s: together with Sherlocs and SPO-15Ms, they were to play an important role in enabling the Iraqis to avoid USN F-14s in 1991.[14]

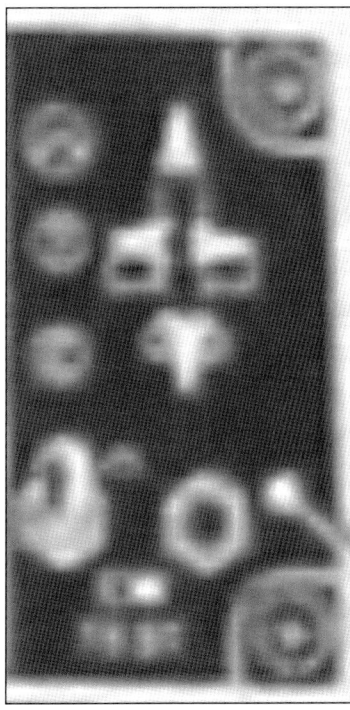

A poor but rare photograph of the Thompson-CSF TMV-011 BF's 'cockpit display': this was the RWR installed into early marks of the Mirage F.1EQ-series. It was roughly comparable not only with the SPO-3 and SPO-10: even the subsequent SPO-15 still used a combination of 'lamps' and aural warnings. (via Antoine Pierre)

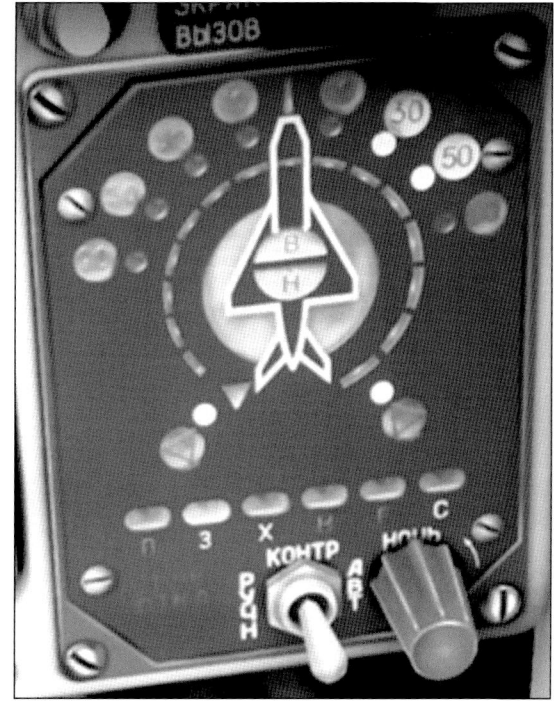

The 'display' of the SPO-15 was slightly more complex than that of the BF, but still consisted of three rows of lamps. While those in the semi-circle around the aircraft symbol identified the direction of the threat, the lower line of lamps would show its nature. (via Ali Tobchi)

industry, which ultimately forced Tehran to accept a UN-mediated cease-fire. Undeniably, it took the IrAF some time to learn how to deploy its Mirages in the most effective fashion, and thus more than 30 were written off in training and combat: by 1990, only 64 single-seaters and 12 two-seaters were still available.[12]

Where the ONI's assessment of the IrAF's Mirage-fleet was closer to reality was the fact that while the type was considered a multi-role platform, the IrAF introduced the practice of specialising its units operating the type. Correspondingly, only two out of four units – Nos. 79 and 89 Squadrons – were assigned the air defence role, while the others were kept back for offensive purposes (see Table 6 for details).

IRAQI FISHBEDS

The balance of the IrAF's interceptor fleet consisted of about a dozen squadrons equipped with a miscellany of about 150 MiG-21 (ASCC/NATO-codename 'Fishbed') point defence interceptors. While more than a half of these belonged to older, hopelessly obsolete variants like the MiG-21F-13, MiG-21FL, MiG-21PFM, and MiG-21MF, the rest were all MiG-21bis, armed with R-60 and R-13M (ASCC/NATO-codename 'AA-2 Atoll') air-to-air missiles. However, after flying nearly 50% of all the combat sorties flown by the IrAF's fixed-wing fleet during the war with Iran, the majority of the fleet was badly worn out and in urgent need of overhauls – if not an outright replacement. Similarly, while the IrAF was also operating about 50 Chinese-made Shenyang F-7 interceptors – based on the design of the MiG-21F-13 – these were never used in combat (and, indeed, never armed), but only as advanced trainers.[13]

TABLE 6: IrAF FIGHTER-INTERCEPTOR UNITS, 1991

UNIT	HQ/BASE	AIRCRAFT TYPE AND NOTES
1st ADS (Centre)	**Taji**	
No. 6 Squadron	Tammuz AB	MiG-29
No. 96 Squadron	Tammuz AB	MiG-25PD; detachment at Jaliba FOB
No. 63 Squadron	Bakr AB	MiG-23ML
No. 93 Squadron	Bakr AB	MiG-23ML
2nd ADS (West)	**Wallid AB**	
No. 39 Squadron	Qaddessiya AB	MiG-29; detachment at Talha FOB
No. 47 Squadron	al-Wallid AB	MiG-21bis
No. 73 Squadron	Sa'ad AB	MiG-23ML
No. 96 Squadron	Qaddessiya AB	MiG-25PD
3rd ADS (South)	**Nassiriyah**	
No. 14 Squadron	Ali Ibn Abu Talib AB	MiG-21bis
No. 11 Squadron	Wahda AB	MiG-21MF
No. 79 Squadron	Abu Ubaida AB	Mirage F.1EQ-2/EQ-4; detachment at Ali Ibn Abu Talib AB
4th ADS (North)	**Kirkuk**	
No. 9 Squadron	Firnas AB	MiG-21MF, detachment at Abu Ubaida Ibn al-Jarrah AB
No. 37 Squadron	al-Hurrya AB	MiG-21bis
No. 79 Squadron	Saddam AB	Mirage F.1EQ-2/4

KARI IADS[15]

Of course, the IrAF had to build-up a radar network and, indeed, an IADS supported by an automated tactical management system (ATMS) to support this large interceptor fleet. Interestingly, while most of its MiG-21bis, not to mention MiG-23MF/MLs and MiG-25PD/PDS were already all equipped with the Lasour data-links, this system is not known to have ever been used. Instead, Baghdad opted to contract the French company Thompson-CSF for this task. The result was the construction of the Kari IADS & ATMS, which became operational in 1984-1985. The 'brain' of the same was the Air Defence Operations Centre (ADOC), constructed inside a massive fortified facility at the former al-Muthana AB in the Baghdad suburb of Mansour. Operated by the Directorate of Operations, IrAF, the ADOC was responsible for compiling the national strategic and tactical picture, for determining strategic directions and tactical air defence priorities, and could also coordinate the operations of radars, communications, electronic counter-measure systems, manned interceptors, surface-to-air missiles, and anti-aircraft artillery. The Kari was sub-divided into four geographically distributed air defence sectors (ADSs): at the heart of each was a sector operations centre (SOC) for air battle management and up to five intercept operations centres (IOCs). These command posts controlled 28 primary, and some 275 secondary, surveillance radars deployed in approximately 100 sites. Between 15 and 20 were static and equipped with long-range E/F-band (2.6-3GHz) radars such as P-35M and P-37 (ASCC/NATO-codename 'Bar Lock'), supported by PRV-11 (ASCC/NATO-codename 'Side Net') E-band height-finders, augmented by Thomson-CSF TRS.2205 Volex III, Thomson-CSF TRS.2215 and 2230 Tigre-S medium-range 'gap-fillers'.[16]

The ADOC was linked to a well-developed network of electronic warfare sites, including Unit 128 – which was a dedicated communications-intelligence (COMINT) and signals-intelligence-gathering asset. Well-integrated, and highly automated, the Kari enabled the commanders at ADOC in Baghdad to control the air battle over any piece of Iraqi airspace at any time of the day. Furthermore, the ADOC was connected to the SOCs and all 14 major air bases (the HQs of which acted as wing-commands, each controlling up to three or four squadrons of combat or combat-support aircraft), by a multiple and hardened network of fibre-optic cables that provided redundancy. The cables connecting the ADOC and the SOCs linked modems capable of switching between direct land lines, microwave and troposcatter communication links, while the SOCs were linked to the IOCs by similar cables for voice and data. Finally, the IOCs were linked to more than 600 observation posts where operators had hand-held pads in which the observer entered heading, altitude, and formation size data, and then transmitted by pushing a button. Like contemporary Soviet IADS and ATMS, the whole system was designed and laid out to be operated by men with limited secondary education: most of the responsibility lay on the shoulders of the better-educated officers. Unsurprisingly, the Kari was an extremely hierarchical system and damage to key sites and its communication system could render it ineffective.

Supported by surveillance and fire-control radars, and a network of visual observation posts, the SOCs were responsible for battle management using interceptors, SAMs, and anti-aircraft artillery. Each could track up to 120 targets and compiled the regional tactical picture which was relayed to the ADOC. Commanders of every SOC had the right to decide how to engage the target, even the type of intercept and the number of missiles to be fired. The IOCs – usually consisting of two vehicles carrying a container with

A rare photograph showing a group of IrAF ground controllers in front of one of the consoles of the Kari ADOC. (Albert Grandolini Collection)

The Main Building of the Directorate of Operations IrAF, at the former al-Muthanna AB, in the Baghdad suburb of Mansour. (via Ali Tobchi)

necessary command, control and communication equipment and parked inside a concrete shelter – could track only a limited number of targets. While capable of quickly dispersing if necessary, their task was to follow the orders issued by the SOCs and execute the task.

Integrated within the Kari were a total of about 67 SAM sites operated by the IrAF and some of 38 operated by the Army. The centrepieces were older Soviet-made SAM-systems such as Volga and Volkhov (ASCC/NATO-codename 'SA-2 Guideline'), and Neva and Pechora (ASCC/NATO-codename 'SA-3 Goa'). Between 1984 and 1989, Iraq imported enough equipment for 39 SA-2 and 52 SA-3 SAM sites, of which 43 were identified as still operational as of late 1990 and 1991. Their primary task was the protection of military production facilities and three air bases in western Iraq. The Air Force's SAM sites were augmented by four French-made Roland SAM-battalions deployed for protection of military and civilian sites, and six battalions equipped with Soviet-made 2K12 Kub (ASCC/NATO-codename 'SA-6 Gainful'), which were assigned to shield the missile sites of the Surface-to-Surface Missile Directorate (SSMD) and al-Wallid AB near the border with Jordan. In addition to SAMs, the Iraqis deployed 7,600 anti-aircraft artillery pieces, including up to 1,800 in Baghdad alone. These ranged from heavy 130mm KS-30 flak to 14.5mm machine guns – the latter often positioned on rooftops or 10-13ft (3-5m) tall earth berms.[17]

A FORCE-IN-BEING

Overall, the IrAF of 1990 was a combat-proven service – theoretically – at the peak of its capabilities, based on immense investment into new equipment and fine-tuned by the long war with Iran. Ironically, at this crucially important moment in time, it was nobody less than Iraqi President Saddam Hussein at-Tikriti – the very man that authorised the massive investment into the Iraqi air power of the 1980s – that effectively castrated the IrAF.

Ever since the 1960s, the commander of the IrAF was supported by four deputies, all with the rank of major-general. The most important amongst these was the Deputy Operations: a major-general in charge of the Directorate of Operations and thus the above-mentioned ADOC. Essentially, together with the Kari IADS & ATMS, this was the 'operational brain' of the air force that controlled all the units equipped with ground-attack, fighter and transport aircraft, as well as all personnel-related affairs. This position was usually occupied by an officer with a background of serving on fighter-bombers. The second most important was the Deputy Air Defence: the officer in charge of the Directorate of Air Defences – which was assigned to the ADOC. This position was usually occupied by a former interceptor pilot, who supervised all air defence activities, including interceptors, SAMs, and anti-aircraft artillery.

In 1988, the long-serving commander of the Air Force, Lieutenant-General Hamid Sha'ban at-Tikriti retired from active service. A former Hunter pilot trained in Great Britain, Sha'ban was an energetic, aggressive officer who commanded the air force not only in the period 1984-1988, when he organised and ran the crucial campaign of strategic bombardment of the Iranian economy, but also in the period 1976-1980, when he played the critical role in purchasing most of the aircraft, armament and weaponry operated by the IrAF as of 1990. Instead of following the tradition based on decades of experience and enabling Sha'ban's logical replacement through appointment of his Deputy Operations, Major-General Salim Sultan al-Basu – the mastermind of the aerial offensive that broke the back of the Iranian capability to continue the war against Iraq – Saddam picked one of his cronies and relatives as the new commander. In early 1989, he appointed his cousin and a former MiG-21 pilot, Colonel Muzahim Sa'ab al-Hassan at-Tikriti as the new commander IrAF.[18]

This – politically-motivated – decision resulted in a major weakening of the Iraqi air force at a crucial point in time. While

IN THE CLAWS OF THE TOMCAT: US NAVY F-14 TOMCATS IN AIR COMBAT AGAINST IRAN AND IRAQ, 1987–2000

As of July-August 1987, only two F-4Es of the 91st TFS, IRIAF were flyable, and only one of them had a fully operational radar and fire-control system. The aircraft of this unit belonged to the final batch of 36 F-4Es acquired by Iran (US FY-serials 75-0222 to 75-0257), and all wore the standardised 'Asia Minor' camouflage pattern, including tan (FS 30400), dark brown (FS30140), and dark green (FS34079) on top surfaces and sides, and USAF light grey (FS36622) on undersurfaces. The sources are unclear, but the F-4E crewed by Major Darious Kaknegar-Moghadam and Captain Mahdi Shaghayegh on 8 August 1987 may have been 75-0256 (IRIAF serial 3-6687). Most likely, it was armed with four AIM-9J Sidewinders and two AIM-7E-2 Sparrows (the latter installed in rear underfuselage bays), as shown here. Inset is shown the patch of the 91st TFS. (Artwork by Tom Cooper)

The F-14As of VF-21 Freelancers somehow evaded the general 'toning down' of their colours in the mid-1980s: most were painted in the 'interim' paint scheme of light gull gray (FS16440) overall, with a large 'anti-glare panel' in front and around the cockpit in matt black, and yellow markings on the fin. Originally the wingman in the section of two was the F-14A BuNo 161607, Modex NK202, flown by LT William 'Bear' Ferran. With his AWG-9 having a better track of the target, and following the Navy's 'loose duce' tactics, Ferran took over the lead and fired a total of two Sparrows during the engagement on 8 August 1987. The first was an AIM-7F (recognisable from an M on its body, painted in white): the second an AIM-7M. The latter missile was evaded by a hard break by Kaknegar-Moghadam, but detonated metres behind his F-4E, spraying the horizontal stabilators with shrapnel. This jet went on to serve with VF-41 and became the first Tomcat to release air-to-ground ordnance during Operation Deliberate Force, over Bosnia, on 1 September 1995. (Artwork by Tom Cooper)

The lead in the section of two VF-21 F-14As to engage the lonesome Iranian F-4E on 8 August 1987 was the F-14A BuNo 161625, Modex NK213, flown by LCDR Robert Clement. Like NK202, it was painted in light gull gray overall, and wore the colourful markings of the squadron. As far as is known, on 8 August 1987 this jet was armed with four AIM-7M Sparrows, and two AIM-9L Sidewinders. Clement stopped guiding his Sparrow before it could hit the target. The subsequent career of this TARPS-capable jet was rather short: it crashed near NAS North Island while operated by VF-111, on 2 August 1989. (Artwork by Tom Cooper)

The most advanced version of the MiG-21 in service with the IrAF as of 1991 was the MiG-21bis, most of which were manufactured and delivered between 1981 and 1984. Nearly all were painted in Soviet colours based on the British Standard 381C system, including beige (BS381C/388) and olive drab (BS381C/298) on top surfaces and sides – applied to a, theoretically, standardised pattern but in a very different fashion to the most common of which (depicted here) was nick-named 'horns' – and light admiralty grey (BS381C/697) on undersurfaces. They were usually armed either with four R-13Ms (ASCC/NATO-codename AA-2D Advanced Atoll, shown on inboard underwing pylon), or with 2 R-13Ms and either two or four R-60s (AA-8 Aphid). Many wore kill markings from the war with Iran, including this example from No. 11 Squadron, destroyed by US Army troops at Jaliba FOB in late March 1991. (Artwork by Tom Cooper)

The leader of the VF-103's MiG-sweep over H-3 on the morning of 17 January 1991, CDR Brian 'Rocky' Fitzpatrick, with LCDR Dana Dervay as RIO, flew this F-14A+, BuNo 163215, Modex AA204. The jet was originally painted in the late style tactical camouflage pattern (TPS), consisting of ghost gray (FS36375) on undersurfaces and sides of engine nacelles, and medium gray (FS35237) on top sides. The latter colour was also applied down the upper half of the forward fuselage, with a sharp demarcation border – that was heavily worn out and thus significantly softened after months of intensive service during operations Desert Shield and Desert Storm, and then 'corrected' in multiple spots through the anti-corrosion measures of the crew. The jet was armed with two AIM-9Ms (notably: VF-74 and VF-103 seem to have been issued with a batch of missiles with their bodies in white), two AIM-7Ms and two AIM-54Cs during that mission: it continued serving with VF-103 well into the 1990s. (Artwork by Tom Cooper)

As Fitzpatrick's MiG-sweep was withdrawing to the south, it was pursued by a pair of MiG-21bis from No. 47 Squadron. The leader of the Navy's division attempted to hand over the engagement to a pair of F-14A+s from VF-74. The lead jet was BuNo 162919, Modex AA101, crewed by Charles 'Cuddles' Wyatt (XO VF-74) and LTJG Craig 'Pep' Peppe: although still relatively new, the jet suffered a break-down of its AWG-9 on take-off, and Peppe's intensive efforts to recover it were only partially successful. As a consequence, neither the lead nor the wingman opened fire at the Iraqi MiGs. Wyatt and Peppe's F-14A+ 162919 was delivered to the Navy only in August 1988, and was still wearing its full TPS, including light ghost gray (FS36375) on undersurfaces, medium gray (FS35237) on sides of the forward fuselage and fins, and dark ghost gray (FS36320) on top sides. (Artwork by Tom Cooper)

The next type of Iraqi interceptor encountered by Navy fighters on 17 January was the MiG-29 (9.12B). As of 1991, the IrAF had two squadrons equipped with the type: No. 6 (the insignia of which, containing Iraqi and Palestinian flags, is shown inset), and No. 39. All wore the standardised camouflage pattern in grey overall, with grey-blue-green splotches on upper surfaces (with slight differences from aircraft to aircraft). As usual for the time after 1989, they wore five-digit serial numbers, always starting with type's designation and applied on the intake. This example, 29040, was one of up to a dozen modified through the installation of the French-made Remora ECM-pod: it remains unclear if this was carried only on the left inboard station, or could also be carried on the right. Both inboard stations were also plumbed to carry drop tanks. In turn, the launch rails for R-27R missiles were moved to the centre underwing stations, while those outboard remained occupied with R-60s. (Artwork by Tom Cooper)

The MiG-sweep for the combined strike by CVW-3 and CVW-17 on H-2 and H-3, later on 17 January 1991, was led by CDR Bob 'Sundance' Davis, CO VF-32. While the exact Tomcat flown by him during that mission remains unknown, the F-14A officially assigned to Davis had a particularly interesting look at the time. Originally, this jet was painted in gull gray overall, with a big anti-glare panel' in front and around the cockpit, and both fins in dark blue, and colourful markings of the VF-32 Swordsmen. Shortly before the commencement of Operation Desert Storm, it received a camouflage pattern consisting of water-soluble ghost grey (FS36320) overall, applied with brushes in a rather crude fashion. The canopy frame and fins received only a thin coat of this colour and were thus significantly darker than the rest of the aircraft: while most national markings and warning insignia were covered, the sword on the fin was still clearly to be seen. In turn, the colour was quickly scratched away immediately below the cockpit, showing the original gull gray. (Artwork by Tom Cooper)

The other squadron involved in the combined CVW-3 and CVW-17 attack on H-2 and H-3 on 17 January 1991 was VF-14. This unit flew some of the oldest F-14As involved in operations Desert Shield and Desert Storm – primarily recognisable by their short UHF/Tacan and UHF/IFF/data-link antennas on the spine, intermediate gun bay vents, and the lack of AN/ALQ-126 housings under the wing gloves (introduced starting with the aircraft of Block 110). Originally, this jet wore the full TPS, including light ghost gray (FS36375) on lower surfaces and sides, medium gray (FS35237) on sides of the forward fuselage and fins, and dark ghost gray (FS36320) on top surfaces, but much of the latter was bleached by the sun. As usual during the first days of the Second Persian Gulf War, its armament consisted of 'two each' of AIM-7M Sparrows, AIM-9M Sidewinders, and AIM-54C Phoenix missiles, in addition to the internally installed 20mm M61A1 Vulcan cannon. (Artwork by Tom Cooper)

All Iraqi Foxbats were painted in medium grey overall (similar to BS381C/626 camouflage grey or FS26152), with all dielectric surfaces (radomes, antenna covers etc.) in dark gull grey (FS26231), and the big anti-glare panel in front of the cockpit in flat black (FS27039). The lower surfaces and sides of the engine nacelles were left in 'natural steel'. Roundels were applied in six positions, while the serials were in black and applied on the forwards fuselage only. The aircraft is shown armed with R-40 (AA-6 Acrid) missiles, which all available Iraqi sources stress were the only weaponry deployed by the type, despite availability of (much smaller and lighter) R-60s: the IR-homing variant was always installed on inboard pylons. Notable is the huge, 5,000-litre drop tank installed on the centreline, which could be carried only by (newly built) MiG-25PDs. Inserts show the insignia of No. 96 Squadron and the position of the national insignia on top wing surfaces. (Artwork by Tom Cooper)

Although USN F-14 crews had a number of encounters with Libyan Foxbats in the 1981-1986 period, it was only on the evening of 17 January 1991 that an F-14A+ of VF-103 became the first Tomcat ever to open fire at what was certainly its most dangerous opponent of the time: an Iraqi MiG-25. This happened when LT Tim 'Glaze' Glaser and RIO LT Alan 'Radar' Metcalfe flew a MiG-sweep for a formation of A-6Es from VA-35 underway to strike the H-3 air base: while a matter of significant controversy and intensive investigation by the USN at the time, this action almost certainly resulted in a (hard) kill that was never officially confirmed. Glaze and Radar's mount was the BuNo 161440 (Modex AA207): the tenth F-14A modified to the F-14A+ standard through the installation of F110-GE-440 engines: a jet that, for quite a while during Operation Desert Shield, had a replacement radome installed, painted in gull gray on top surfaces and sides, and white at the bottom. (Artwork by Tom Cooper)

This Tomcat – BuNo 161430 – was the twenty-second F-14A retrofitted to F-14A+ standard and then delivered to VF-103 in May 1990: less than a year later, it became the eleventh aircraft of the Coalition, and the third of CVW-17, to be shot down by the Iraqis. Whether it was felled by an SA-2, as officially concluded by the USN and the IrAF, or by an Iraqi MiG-29 still remains unclear: the crew ejected safely and the pilot was recovered a few hours later, but the RIO ended the conflict as a prisoner of war in Iraq. Originally painted in the TPS, with ghost gray and medium gray on undersurfaces and sides, respectively, by January 1991 most of the dark ghost gray colour on its top surfaces was bleached by the sun and salt water. It is shown in configuration as during its final flight, including armament consisting of two AIM-9Ms (with white bodies), two AIM-7Ms, and two AIM-54Cs. (Artwork by Tom Cooper)

The next Tomcat to clash with Foxbats was BuNo 162925, Modex AA100, flown by LT Scott 'Shaggy' Alwine and LCDR Dan 'Tarps' Cloyd early on 21 January 1991. Only minutes after the loss of VF-103's AA212, they found themselves under attack by an Iraqi MiG-25, managed to outmanoeuvre it and gain a favourable position behind it. With the AWACS failing to provide a positive identification in time, Alwine and Cloyd lost a near-certain kill when the Iraqi realised his predicament and dived into the clouds. As of January 1991, this F-14A+ wore the same version of the TPS as most of the other Tomcats of VF-74, including light ghost gray and medium gray, with most of the dark ghost gray being bleached by the sun and elements. The weapon configuration during this mission consisted of 'two each', as depicted here. The jet went on to serve with VF-102 and participate in air strikes on Bosnian Serbs in 1995. (Artwork by Tom Cooper)

The last F-14A from the carriers deployed in the Red Sea known to have had a 'MiG-contact' during Operation Desert Storm was this example: the F-14A 162705, Modex AB201. While pursuing a pair of MiG-29s on 27 January 1991, the CO VF-33, CDR Dale O. Snodgrass ran into a SAM-trap. Still loaded with two AIM-7Ms, two AIM-9Ms and two AIM-54Cs, the jet lost one engine and almost fell into a spin, requiring all of the pilot's knowledge to recover. Notably, while a relatively new jet, already equipped with the final version of gun bay vents and the AN/ALQ-126, the jet still had short UHF/Tacan and UHF/IFF/data-link antennas. Originally, it wore a full TPS, but nearly all of the dark gull gray colour on its top surfaces was bleached by the sun and washed out by the rain and sea water. (Artwork by Tom Cooper)

With the exception of a few Mirage F.1EQ-5s camouflaged suitably for maritime operations, all the Iraqi Mirage F.1s wore a standardised camouflage pattern in Brun Café (dark sand, FS30475) and Khaki (FS36134) on top surfaces and sides, and light blue-grey (FS35189) on undersurfaces. Underwing hardpoints and the 2,000-litre Irakien drop tank were left in natural metal overall. National markings were worn in six positions, while the Mirages retained their original four-digit serial numbers applied before delivery. The F.1EQ-4 was the first variant equipped for IFR and had a corresponding probe on the right side in front of the cockpit. The fate of the jet shown here remains unknown, but it is configured as the two F.1EQ-4s sent on the al-Abaqiq strike, including one SAMP 400kg bomb under each of the underwing hardpoints and two wing-tip installed R.550 Magic air-to-air missiles. The inset shows the crest of No. 81 Squadron, IrAF. (Artwork by Tom Cooper)

One of two F-14As from VF-84 patrolling the Whiskey 4 CAP-station at the time of the Iraqi air strike on al-Abaqiq, on 24 January, was BuNo 161164, Modex AJ211, the RIO of which on that day is known to have been LT John Martins. The jet wore a worn out TPS applied in similar fashion to that on Tomcats from VF-74 and VF-103, but with the lower border of the medium gray slightly higher, and almost completely washed out dark gull gray. On 24 January 1991, it was configured in the standard 'two each' weapons configuration. VF-84, and sister-squadron VF-41, flew combat sorties from the Red Sea and from the Persian Gulf, before moving into the Mediterranean – after Operation Desert Storm – from where it flew some of the first sorties in control of the northern NFZ. This TARPS-configured Tomcat continued serving with VF-32 and then VF-211 well into the 1990s. (Artwork by Tom Cooper)

'Wichita 103' was the tactical call-sign of F-14A, BuNo 162603, the Tomcat flown by LT Stuart 'Meat' Broce and CDR Ron 'Bongo' McElraft on 6 February 1991, when they shot down an Iraqi Mi-17 helicopter. While widely claimed as the 'only' kill, this was most likely the second kill scored by Tomcats during the Second Gulf War. Because initial intelligence reports cited an 'Mi-24' as its target, the jet – painted in gull gray overall – was decorated with a kill marking comprising a silhouette of that type, applied between the canopy rails and the national marking. The weapons configuration was typical for the times late during this conflict and consisted of four AIM-9Ms and four AIM-7Ms. (Artwork by Tom Cooper)

All the Iraqi MiG-23MLs were camouflaged in the standardised pattern for export aircraft, consisting of beige (BS381C/388), dark brown (BS381C/411 or 450, similar to FS20095), and olive drab (BS381C/298, similar to FS34098), on the upper surfaces. Undersurfaces were in light admiralty grey (BS381C/697 or FS35622). National markings were worn in six positions, with those on upper and bottom wing surfaces pointing 'straight ahead' when the aircraft was parked with wings fully swept back. Starting in 1989, their serials were changed from a four-digit to a five-digit system, starting with the type's designation. Correspondingly, this jet – originally 5270 – became 23270. Notable is the installation of the Remora ECM-pod low under the fuselage, SRO-15 RWR atop the fin, and the ASO-2 chaff and flare dispenser (taken from Sukhoi Su-22M-4s) atop the centre fuselage. Inset is shown the crest of No. 93 Squadron, IrAF. (Artwork by Tom Cooper)

All the F-14Ds were delivered to the Navy already painted in the TPS consisting of light ghost gray (FS36375), medium gray (FS35237) on sides and fins, and dark ghost gray (FS36320) on top sides. Moreover, during the 1990s, very few wore any of the more colourful markings for which the US naval aviation had been famous at earlier times. The sole exception to such rules was equipment like Phoenix pallets: many were manufactured at earlier times and thus painted in light gull gray. This jet, BuNo 163903, Modex NH107, was flown by LCDR Vince 'Bluto' Sparito and LCDR Bob 'Jumby' Castleton when they engaged an Iraqi MiG-25PD/PDS on 5 January 1991. By this time, the standard weapons configuration included one AIM-7M Sparrow, two AIM-9M Sidewinders, and one AIM-54C Phoenix. (Artwork by Tom Cooper)

The second Tomcat to release an AIM-54C on 5 January 1991 was the F-14D(R) BuNo 159619. The aircraft was crewed by LT Jonathan 'Shoe' Shoemaker and LT Mike 'BuFi' Bilzor. The jet also wore the full TPS at the time, but this was slightly more washed out than on the NH107. Like the Phoenix released by 'Lion 107', the missile's motor failed to ignite because it was not armed before the catapult launch. The two F/A-18Cs that attempted to catch the pair of MiG-23MLs included BuNo 164012/NH314, flown by LCDR Tim 'Drac' Aslin, and BuNo 163092/NH207, flown by LCDR Neil 'Waylon' Jennings. (Artwork by Tom Cooper)

The last ever USN Tomcat to engage in air combat was the F-14AD BuNo 164349, Modex NE102, assigned to the oldest of the Navy's fighter squadrons: VF-2 Bounty Hunters, a unit that had the tradition of applying the 'Langley Strip' on its aircraft. During the 1990s, the latter was usually applied in three shades of grey on the fin, instead of dark blue, white and red, below the cockpit. On 14 September 1999, this Tomcat was crewed by LCDR Coby 'Coach' Loessberg and LCDR Michael 'Spock' McMillan, who released a single AIM-54C at a pair of Iraqi MiG-23MLs violating the southern NFZ. The missile prompted both Floggers into a rapid turn followed by acceleration to supersonic speed that brought them outside the AIM-54C's engagement envelope. (Artwork by Tom Cooper)

A map of Iraq with the Kari IADS and ATMS – and thus the primary battlefield for USN F-14s and IrAF interceptors as of 1990-1998. Notably, during the occupation of Kuwait, in 1990-1991, a fifth air defence sector was added to the original four: this had no flying units assigned though. (Map by Tom Cooper)

Saddam's influence did not end with the choice of the commanders of the Iraqi air force but extended to the selection of squadron commanders. The Commander IrAF of 1991, General Muzahim Sa'ab al-Hassan at-Tikriti (centre, browsing a handbook) was a highly experienced MiG-21 pilot, but lacked the knowledge and understanding for actual capabilities of the force he was supposed to command. Similarly, the few former MiG-25 pilots available for at least brief interviews have indicated that the CO No. 96 Squadron (in flight overall, to the right of Muzahim) was selected for his relations to the president of Iraq, rather than merits. (via Ali Tobchi)

The former Squadron Building of No. 96 Squadron at Tammuz AB, seen in November 2020. (Photo by Mohammed al-Jassim)

who was always and exclusively an Army officer, and that the Iraqi Army generals had no clear understanding of the capabilities of modern air power. Finally, there are strong indications that, just like Hassan, his new deputies also had no clear knowledge of the actual capabilities of all the aircraft, equipment, and personnel of the IrAF as of 1988-1990.[19]

DEFENSIVE STRATEGY

Overall, at a crucial point in time, the IrAF was left essentially leaderless, and thus ill-prepared for what it was about to face. All of this mattered very little to Saddam: while justifiably proud of the IrAF, he was a strong believer in the 'fleet in being' philosophy. From his point of view, it did not matter if the air force could not operate effectively, as long as it was well-equipped and existent, and its personnel were loyal to him. The longer the Kuwait crisis lasted, the more obvious it became that there was going to be a war, and that the IrAF would find itself facing a vastly superior enemy. As a result, the air force adopted a defensive strategy based upon the use of SAMs and anti-aircraft artillery, while trying to conserve its pilots and aircraft. For all practical purposes, and unknown to the Allies, Baghdad limited the role of its air force to that of surviving the coming war.[20]

certainly a versed MiG-21 pilot, former base-commander, and staff officer fresh from completing higher military education at Egypt's prestigious Gamal Abdel Nasser Academy for Higher Military Studies, Hassan was simply not up to the task. He had flown only point-defence interceptors at earlier times and thus not only lacked experience in commanding complex operations of advanced multi-role aircraft, but also those including multiple formations of mutually-supporting combat-support-aircraft, interceptors, bombers, and fighter-bombers of the kind the IrAF flew regularly during the last two years of war with Iran. Moreover, unlike those of Sha'ban, Hussein's principal aides were also of low calibre: together with Hassan, and contrary to Sha'ban and Basu at earlier times, they all lacked the connections within the High Command in Baghdad necessary to influence the planning of the General Headquarters (GHQ) at strategic and operational levels. This was even more important considering that the position of the commander of the IrAF was subordinated to the Chief-of-Staff of the Armed Forces,

Therefore, instead of trying to openly challenge a superior enemy in the air, the mass of the IrAF's interceptor fleet was held back. About 30 pilots authorised to do more were to scramble and fly to pre-determined control points in 'total emission control' (EMCON) – with their radars turned off, only listening for messages from their ground control, and monitoring their radar warning receivers. Once close to the target the ground control would advise them to activate their radars, after which the pilots were to use their own initiative. The first corresponding exercise was undertaken during the night from 25 to 26 December 1990: it promptly showed that such tactics were impossible to exercise with MiG-25s because they were much too fast. Nevertheless, other IrAF interceptors were to use it. Indeed, all those confirmed as shot down during the subsequent war were lost while not under ground control – if for no other reason than because communications were jammed, or because ground radars were jammed or destroyed.[21]

TOLKACHEV FACTOR

Amid the general trend of patronising any 'Arab' armed forces, and the Iraqi in particular, most publications covering aerial warfare during the Second Persian Gulf War of 1991 overlook a very important 'espionage' affair of the late 1970s and early 1980s.

In 1979, Adolf Georgievich Tolkachev, an electronics engineer who was working as one of the chief designers at the Scientific Research Institute of Radar (NIIR or NII Radar, meanwhile better-known as Phazotron Design Bureau) – the Soviet Union's largest developer of military radars and avionics – became disappointed by the persecution of his wife's parents and the communist rule in general. Correspondingly, he clandestinely established links to the Central Intelligence Agency (CIA) of the USA in Moscow and began transferring immense volumes of highly classified and extremely sensitive data about the most important radars and weapon systems installed in Soviet-made aircraft. The amount of materials Tolkachev provided was such that the CIA translators could not keep up with their task: actually, US intelligence was still busy translating and studying the information supplied by him well into the 1990s, years after he was revealed to the Soviets by one of their spies within the US intelligence community, and arrested, sometime in early 1985. While the CIA never released precise details, the available information emphasised that the intelligence provided by Tolkachev was crucial to the USAF completely re-designing the electronic package for its latest fighter jets in 1979. An internal evaluation by the CIA from March 1980 praised the Russian for providing details of unprecedented quality – and that years before these had entered service. In April 1980, another internal CIA memorandum called his information on jam-proofing tests for Soviet fighter aircraft radar systems 'unique': obviously, he provided data that was not obtainable by any other means. Only a few months later, Tolkachev was credited with, 'providing unique information on a new Soviet fighter aircraft, and documents on several new models of airborne missile systems.' Similarly, a memorandum from the Defence Department from September 1980 praised the impact of Tolkachev's reporting as, 'limitless in terms of enhancing US military systems' effectiveness, and, 'in the potential to save lives and equipment...instrumental in shaping the course of billions of dollars of US research and development activities...'[22]

While Moscow remains zip-lipped about the entire affair to this day, the deduction of related reports is indicative that Tolkachev caused irreparable damage to the Soviet defence sector, and aviation industry in particular. Foremost, he betrayed an entire generation of the latest fighter jets – including the MiG-29, MiG-31, and Su-27 – and their weapon systems, and thus enabled the development of effective electronic countermeasures against them even before they had entered operational service in the 1980s. It is near certain that his treachery played an important role in enabling the USA and allies to defeat the IrAF in 1991, too.

PILOT FACTOR

Most of the future Tomcat crews of the USN were drawn from the Naval Reserve Officer Training Corps program or the US Naval Academy: when not, they had to attend the Aviation Officer Training School. After attending primary flight training at the Naval Air Stations (NAS) Pensacola or Corpus Christi, they would enter advanced training. Their washout rates were low, because just getting into the Primary was extremely selective. Moreover, their subsequent careers depended as much on skills as on the Navy's requirements in the given year: at times it often happened that entire classes were assigned to fly transports, or early warning aircraft, it did take some luck to be selected for jet training and, after successfully completing this, for Tomcats. The next stop of the future F-14 crews was the Fleet Replacement Squadron, colloquially known as the 'RAG'. As of the 1980s, there were two such units: at NAS Oceana, VF-101 was training future F-14 crews for the Atlantic Fleet, and at NAS Miramar VF-124 for the Pacific Fleet. Once assigned to the two units, the crews went through five extremely intensive and painstaking training phases, which taught them about the systems, basic handling, switchology, and emergency procedures. This was still far from all: further courses on weapons, intercept tactics, radar and communication, electronic countermeasures, and air-to-air gunnery, all lead to the courses in basic fighter manoeuvring and tactics, where students learned how to make the Tomcat the most effective fighter. The ultimate test was carrier qualification, where crews were taught how to land and take-off from an aircraft carrier. After something like a year at the RAG, a pilot or the RIO was ready for his (in the 1980s there were no female F-14 crews) fist active tour with an operational squadron, where they underwent yet additional tactical and operational training, including regular squadron and airwing work-ups prior to, and intensive operational exercises during, every cruise. The Navy never bought dual-control F-14s all the way from the RAG into operational squadrons, there was a policy of pairing 'nuggets' – new pilots or RIOs – with highly experienced RIOs or pilots. The concept was that of enabling senior officers to forward their hard-won experience to junior officers, and it worked small miracles, then the high tempo of operations in an extremely dangerous environment subjected everybody's skills to constant critique and testing. While the USN considered its F-14s foremost as 'fleet defenders' – and, indeed, Tomcat squadrons primarily expected to operate over the water during any kind of a war – it took exceptional care to train their crews in all imaginable regimes of air combat. Therefore, as much emphasis was put on close-in air combat manoeuvring as on air combat in the BVR-regime. Where there was a major difference to the IrAF was that there was next to no combat experience: instead, top Navy air warfare tacticians of the 1980s had to depend on experiences from exercises and theory for their theses.

Never a topic attracting lots of public attention at home or abroad, but always a subject of entirely unsubstantiated patronising (and lots of prejudice) by the West, Iraqi fighter pilots of 1990-1991 were actually a group of seasoned combat veterans, with particularly extensive experience in air combat in the BVR-regime. All future Iraqi fighter pilots were graduates of the Air Force Academy in Tikrit. Once having earned their wings, they underwent fighter

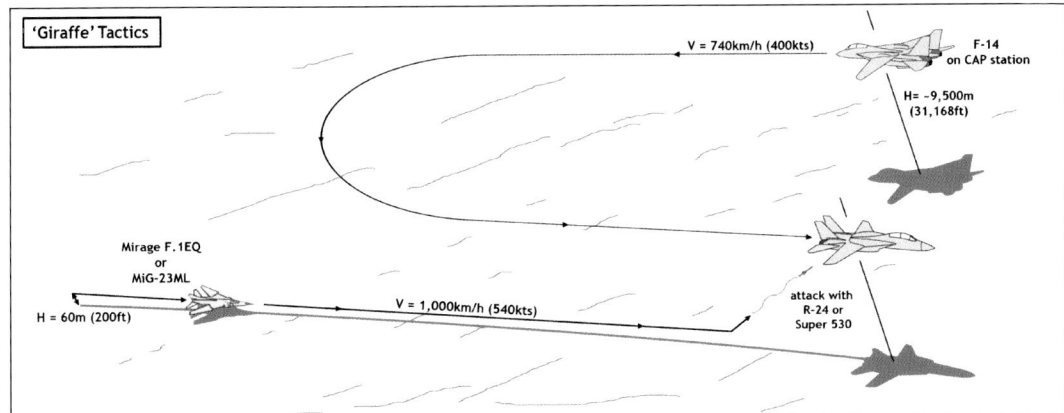

Based on experience from the war with Iran, the principal Iraqi tactic against the F-14 was called the 'Giraffe'. Originally, it consisted of the approach of two pairs of Mirages and/or MiG-23MF/MLs at very low altitude from two different directions as the Tomcats were on the 'return leg' of their racetrack CAP-pattern. It was in this fashion that the IrAF Mirages shot down three Iranian F-14s in 1981, and MiG-23MLs in 1984. The Iranians countered it – with quite some success – by positioning low-flying F-5Es in front of the Tomcats. (Diagram by Tom Cooper)

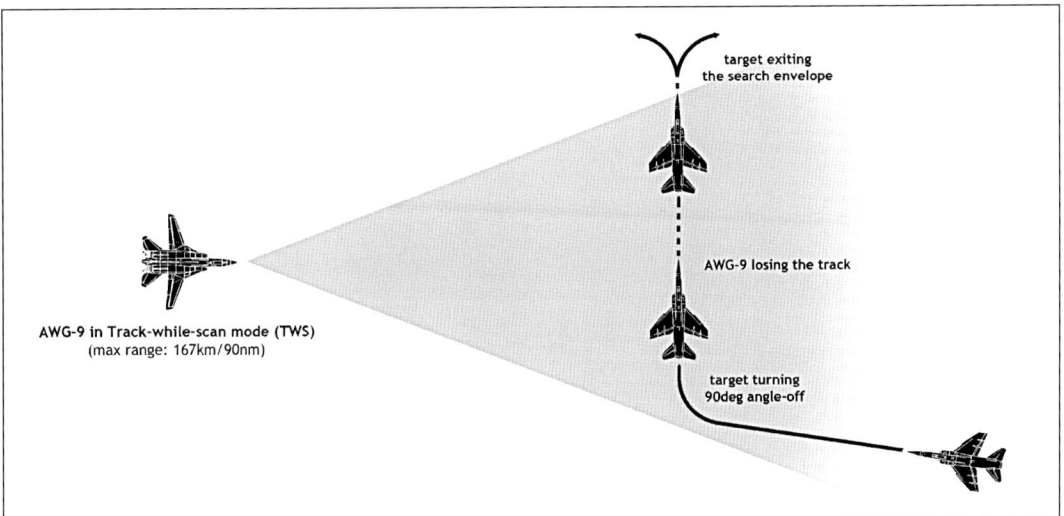

The principal Iraqi anti-Tomcat manoeuvre became known as 'Beaming' or 'Notching'. As the ONI assessed in SPEARTIP 014-90, '…it appears they became aware of the limitations of the F-14's high PRF mode in the beam…' In a (massive) oversimplification, this manoeuvre exploited the fact that the processor of the AWG-9 filtered out targets having zero relative motion in comparison to the Tomcat carrying it. Therefore, whenever their RWR warned them of an AWG-9, the Iraqi pilots would turn perpendicular to the threat with the aim of breaking the lock on. (Diagram by Tom Cooper)

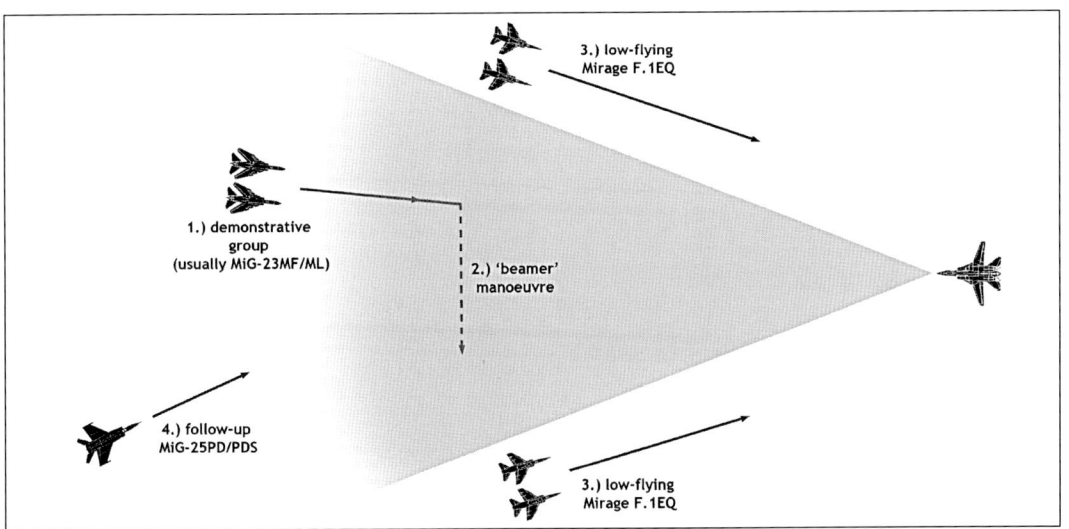

From 1984, the Giraffe tactics were refined and the Iraqis began deploying one or two pairs of MiG-23MLs as decoys: they would show themselves and 'drag' Tomcats to get other fighters unseen and undetected within range of their Super 530s (on Mirage F.1EQs), R-24s (on MiG-23MLs), or even R-40s (on MiG-25s). Deploying these tactics, the Iraqi MiG-25s shot down one Iranian Tomcat in 1987, while Mirages damaged another in 1988. (Diagram by Tom Cooper)

conversion courses on Chinese-made Shenyang F-7s, before undergoing conversion courses to specific fighter-interceptor types. Most future MiG-23 and MiG-25 pilots used to serve at least one tour in MiG-21 units; it was only during the second half of the war with Iran, that an ever larger number of pilots emerged completely trained in France, and trained to fly Mirage F.1s from the start. The majority of Iraqi MiG-29 pilots used to fly MiG-23s at earlier times.

Even if not of the same intensity and quality, their flight and tactical training was as throughout as that provided to US Navy aviators. The fundamental differences were higher washout rates, and that the training in close-in air combat manoeuvring was far less intensive, consisting of more theoretic lessons than air combat manoeuvring exercises. The reason was that the experience from eight years of war with Iran – during which they fought not just a handful, but hundreds of air combats – taught Iraqis that the mass of modern-day aerial engagements was fought – and decided – by semi-active radar homing medium-range air-to-air missiles, nearly always deployed from beyond visual range. This came not for nothing: not only the mass of IrAF Mirage pilots claimed all of their kills against Iranians with the Super 530D missile, but the Iraqi MiG-23 and MiG-25 pilots next to never used their R-60s. Indeed, even the few MiG-29 pilots that flew the type in combat during the last year of the war with Iran, only ever deployed R-27 air-to-air missiles. Foremost, the Iraqis learned (initially: the hard way) about what the F-14 could and could not do: even if only very few would ever admit it openly, they were aware of the fact that the issue of countering Iranian Tomcats gradually reached strategic proportions:

MISSION FOX

The longer the Kuwait crisis went on, the more the Navy learned about the IrAF, the more serious the threat of Iraqi interceptors was assessed to be. When it became obvious there would be a war, the USN took care to organise dissimilar air combat exercises against aircraft operated by the Iraqis – like MiG-29s in Germany (freshly inherited from the former East German air force), and like Mirage F.1EQs in France. A group of crews from CVW-17 was sent to Europe for this purpose, together with two F-14A+s from VF-103, and four F/A-18s from VFA-81 and VF-83 in September 1990. Amongst others in France, they flew training missions against two undelivered Mirage F.1EQ-5/6s (serials 4562 and 4662). After returning to the Red Sea, these crews then toured all the aircraft carriers in the sea to share their experiences. Scott Alwine recalled the resulting impressions:

… the MiG-29 with its air-to-air missiles, especially the [R-73/AA-11] Archer, was a formidable threat and our primary air-to-air concern. Iraqi crews had been fighting Iranians for years and we knew they knew tricks: we were worried about such tactics like launching MiG-21s from roads beneath our formation, where our radars couldn't see them. An experienced crew in an F-14A+ could do well against a MiG-29, and our squadrons used [the] Navy's F-16s to make sure we were ready for that kind of engagement….I remember being told that there would be 480 Coalition aircraft in the country in the early hours of the war and we could expect up to 30% losses….we expected a lots of air-to-air action and possible turning engagement … more senior crews thus put themselves on the sweep missions pre-war, while juniors were left with HVU-escort duty.[26]

In September 1990, the French used the undelivered Mirage F.1EQ-5 serial number 4562 – which also served as a prototype for the ultimate F.1EQ-6 variant – for training several F-14 and F/A-18 crews of CVW-17. The Americans were primarily interested in finding out from what range its Cyrano-IVQ radar could detect their aircraft, and about the effectiveness of their ECM. Unsurprisingly, all the photographs taken during that exercise show the Iraqi F.1EQ toting at least one Remora ECM-pod – developed on Iraqi order to counter the AWG-9 radar of the F-14. (Photo by Jean-Francois Lipka)

Ironically, one of CVW-17's jets deployed during Operation Mission Fox to France in September-October 1990 was the F/A-18C BuNo 163484, Modex AA403 – the very aircraft shot down by an Iraqi MiG-25 Foxbat, on the early morning of 17 January 1991. (Photo by M. Jean-Jacques Petit)

after many negative experiences from the 1980-1982 period, it prompted the government in Baghdad (deeply impressed by the F-14 ever since Iran placed its first order for these) into spending an equivalent of more than US$1 billion to pay the French to develop suitable electronic countermeasures. By 1985, the deployment and availability of these was a matter of 'go' or 'no go' for the mass of IrAF operations against Iran. As a result, not only was the IrAF far better equipped for this task than could have been expected from the mass of other air forces around the world, but it also had more pilots with current or recent experience in fighting in the BVR-regime, than anybody else. In other words: far from being 'noobs', even Iraqi MiG-21 pilots were well-versed in countering the F-14, while their MiG-23, MiG-25, MiG-29 and Mirage F.1 pilots were some of the most dangerous opponents the Navy's Tomcat crews could face under combat conditions at the time.²³

DELAY AND DISRUPT DOCTRINE

Finally, a few words ought to be said about the US Navy's fighter doctrine of 1991. Reading the content of the following chapter might create the impression of this being 'too conservative'. However, one should keep in mind that there were plenty of excellent reasons why. Primary amongst these was that the doctrine of the US Navy was that of fighting a war against the USSR by striking its major bases on the Kola Peninsula and in the Far East. Because no allies could operate in such a high-threat areas, operations there were to be run by the Navy alone. Moreover, the available intelligence indicated that, despite all its quirks and weak spots, the F-14 provided the USN with such vast technological superiority in comparison to whatever was likely to come its way at the time, that the type was likely to decide the mass of its engagements through deterrent and intimidation alone, and would do so during operations over the sea, without crossing the enemy coast. Although this was never written in the Navy's original requirement for the AWG-9, AIM-54, or the F-14, this superiority was of such quality that in any war the type was near-certain to score far more 'mission kills' through forcing its opponent away by its sheer presence, or even grounding them, than to actually shoot down its opponents. In other words – and as proven by the operations of Iranian Tomcats during the war with Iraq – the Tomcat did not require scoring 50, 100, 150 or more 'kills' to become successful.²⁴

Unsurprisingly, the Topgun courses of the late 1980s taught not only F-14 crews, but also squadron commanders (COs) and deputy commanders (XOs), airwing staff and even CVBG commanders, that the job of Tomcats during offensive operations was to stay with the strike package – with fighter-bombers, electronic warfare and other aircraft they were supposed to protect – to 'delay and disrupt', instead of 'chasing MiGs'. This even more so because in combat there was always the chance of the enemy deploying a demonstrative group of aircraft to decoy F-14s away, and then hitting the strike package they were supposed to protect. The intensive and thorough training of USN Tomcat crews resulted in this idea sinking into everybody to a degree where it greatly influenced their planning for and conduct of operations against Iraq in 1991. As a result, in thousands of sorties flown by F-14s during 42 days of the Second Persian Gulf War, not one F-14 crew decided to abandon the formation it was tasked with protecting, regardless what was going on around it, or what kind of threat was it facing.²⁵

5
TOMCAT AT WAR

The overall war plan for Operation Desert Storm envisaged a weeklong onslaught on the Kari IADS & ATMS, followed by attacks on other targets. The assault on the Kari was to start with US Army helicopters knocking out Iraqi early warning radars along the border with Saudi Arabia. This blow was to create a 'corridor' in the enemy radar network through which BGM-109 Tomahawk Land Attack Missiles (TLAMs) of the USN and Lockheed F-117A stealth fighters of the USAF were to reach heavily protected command nodes in the Baghdad area. They were to be followed by F-15E Strike Eagle fighter-bombers – protected by Grumman EF-111A electronic warfare aircraft – that were to hit enemy ballistic missile units in western Iraq. Subsequently, other aircraft – including those of the USN – were to unleash an unprecedented aerial campaign against Iraqi leadership and military command nodes, while at the same time targeting primary air defence facilities and air bases, units operating ballistic missiles, and other major military bases.

This entire enterprise was so massive, and undertaken over such ranges, that it was entirely dependent on the availability of tanker aircraft: the USAF deployed over 160 Boeing KC-135 Stratotankers and McDonnell-Douglas KC-10A Extenders to Saudi Arabia, and these were reinforced by tankers of the RAF. However, that was still not enough. Correspondingly, initial operations against Iraq

USS *Saratoga* with aircraft of CVW-17 on the deck, seen in 1990: Tomcats from this airwing were to see most of the air-to-air action during the war with Iraq.

were to see the involvement of the aircraft from USN aircraft carriers *Saratoga*, *Kennedy*, *Ranger* and *Midway*, only. Moreover, USS *America* had only arrived on station in the Red Sea and was too late to be included in the original air tasking order (ATO) process, while USS *Roosevelt* was still in transit to the Persian Gulf. This is why only the crews of six out of ten F-14 squadrons deployed during Operation Desert Storm were to see combat action early on.[1]

ONSLAUGHT

For the USN, Operation Desert Storm began at 01.30hrs Iraqi time of 17 January 1991, when the guided missile cruiser USS *San Jacinto* (CG-56) fired the first out of six TLAMs from its station in the northern Red Sea: all were aimed at the Ba'ath Party HQ in downtown Baghdad and, because there was no way to re-route them once they were airborne, this was also the moment the USA and its allies became definitely committed to an armed conflict with Iraq. Next into action were Hughes AH-64 Apache attack helicopters of the US Army's Task Force Normandy, which attacked and quickly knocked out two Iraqi early warning radar sites in the Nukhayd area, at 02.50hrs. They were closely followed by F-117As that went after the main command nodes in the Baghdad area, F-15Es that attacked ballistic missile sites in western Iraq, another wave of F-117s, and several General Dynamics EF-111A electronic warfare aircraft. Finally, as all these aircraft began returning to Saudi Arabia, two squadrons of USAF F-15Cs flew a fighter-sweep over southern Iraq, engaging multiple IrAF interceptors as they went. Not letting up, next the CAOC sent a true 'gorilla package' over Iraq: this included over 160 USAF, USN and Royal Air Force (RAF) aircraft that simultaneously pushed from the south-west and south in the direction of Baghdad. Consisting of aircraft from *Kennedy* and *Saratoga*, the Navy's component included:

- 10 F/A-18s (5 from VFA-81 and 5 from VFA-83), armed with AGM-88 HARMs;
- 8 A-6E Intruders (4 from VA-35 and 4 from VA-75), armed with Mk.84 free-fall bombs and GBU-10 laser-guided bombs (LGBs), respectively;
- 10 Vought A-7E Corsair IIs (5 from VA-46 and 5 from VA-72), armed with AGM-88 HARMs and ADM-141s;
- 3 EA-6B Prowlers (VAQ-132), and
- 2 F-14A+s from VF-103 and 1 from VF-74 as 'high-value unit' (HVU) escorts.

FOXBAT RUNNING AMOK

Ironically, for the Tomcat crews operating from carriers in the Red Sea, the war did not start with a traditional MiG-sweep, but with a SEAD effort. Armed with AGM-88 HARM anti-radar missiles and ADM-141 TALD decoy missiles, Hornets and Corsairs flew suppression of enemy air defences (SEAD), and thus were underway at an altitude of 6,100-7,620m (20,000-25,000ft): high enough to

A pair of F-14As from VF-14, passing above USS *Kennedy*, in 1990.

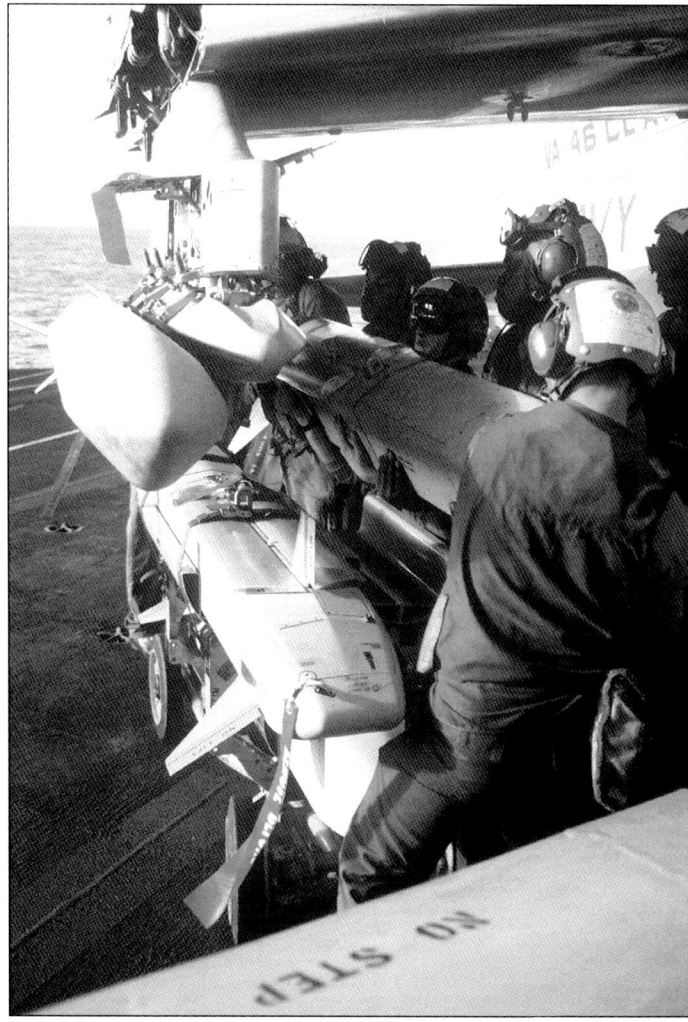

Ordnance specialists of VA-46 loading ADM-141 TALD decoys on an A-7E on the deck of the USS *Kennedy* on 16 January 1991. Each TALD was equipped with passive and active radar enhancers, enabling it to mimic a combat aircraft, and thus confuse and saturate enemy air defences. More than 100 ADM-141s were released during the first night of the war: their unexpected appearance caused a great deal of confusion within the IrAF – and a mass of unsubstantiated claims for shoot-downs, which kept its Intelligence Directorate busy for years after.

attract the attention of enemy radars. Three EA-6B Prowlers, each with one F-14 as escort, then passed by to the east to take three stations in between the Hornets and Baghdad, on north-to-south axis: VF-103 escorted the northern and southern Prowler, the VF-74 the centre one. Not only did this make the work of both crews easier, but the F-14s' loadout of two AIM-54s, three AIM-7s, and two AIM-9s was considered enough for the perceived threat. Approaching behind this 'shield' of electronic warfare aircraft and their escorts, and SEAD assets, A-6Es were to bomb Wallid AB shortly after it had been subjected to a low-altitude strike by four PANAVIA Tornado GR.Mk 1s of the RAF, equipped with JP.233 submunition dispensers.[2]

The Navy formation was picked up by Iraqi radars and ESM-systems before it crossed the border from Saudi Arabia to Iraq, and around 02.30hrs local time, the IrAF ordered four MiG-25s to scramble from Qadessiya and Wallid ABs. The only one that managed to get airborne before both Iraqi bases were hit by low-flying Tornados was the Foxbat piloted by Lieutenant Zuhair Dawoud from No. 96 Squadron. Climbing from Qadessiya in full afterburner, he turned south while accelerating to Mach 1.4, before levelling out at an altitude of 8,000m (26,247ft) and setting his Smerch-A2 radar to standby mode, to warm it up. As the MiG-25PD climbed, it was detected by one of the E-2Cs supporting the Navy's strike package, then the APG-65 of the CO VFA-81, CDR Michael T 'Spock' Anderson (in F/A-18C 163480/AA402), and by the AWG-9s on the F-14A+ Tomcat from VF-74 flown by LT Scott 'Shaggy' Alwine, with LCDR Dan 'Traps' Cloyd as RIO. Anderson not only knew the aircraft ahead of him must be enemy because it was climbing out of an enemy air base, but also because by using the NCTR of his APG-65, he determined it as a foe. As Dawoud approached to about 90km (47nm) from the Hornets, his SPO-15 warned him that an enemy aircraft had locked onto him with radar: he broke hard right to a course perpendicular to the Navy's formation, thus shaking off the lock-on. The fast-climbing and then hard-turning Foxbat was still at the very edge of the AWACS' radar range, and it did not power up its radar and is why the controller on the E-3, call-sign Cougar, orbiting nearly 300 miles south was slow in identifying it. Worse yet, the E-2C controller did so – but on the wrong frequency. Ultimately, neither Anderson nor anybody else opened fire. Undisturbed, Dawoud continued his flight in a western direction, switching off

Zohair Dawoud, the MiG-25 pilot that – nearly – ran amok after finding himself in the left flank of the CVW-17 formation early on 17 January 1991. (via Ali Tobchi)

Zohair Dawoud (left, in g-suit), in front of one of No. 97 Squadron's MiG-25PDSs. (via Ali Tobchi)

The F-14A+ BuNo 163221, Modex AA105 was the jet crewed by Alwine and Cloyd during their HVU-escort mission, early on 17 January 1991.

NAMES OF IRAQI AIR BASES

Because so little was known about the IrAF in the West in 1990-1991, a significant number of different names have been used for various of its bases. For the reader's easier orientation, the following table provides a comparison of US and British designations for major air bases in Iraq.

TABLE 7: IRAQI AIR BASE NAMES AND THEIR FOREIGN DESIGNATIONS, 1991		
US/BRITISH NAME	IrAF NAME	NOTES
Asad/Asssad/al-Assad	Qadessiya	newly constructed in the 1980s; first named al-Baghdadi AB, then re-named after a famous battle in which the Arabs defeated the Persians in 636
Balad	al-Bakr	newly constructed in the 1980s; named after the former Iraqi President Ahmad Hassan al-Bakr
H-1 New	Assad	originally a small airfield near the pumping station on the oil pipeline connecting Kirkuk with Haifa; expanded into a major air base
H-2	Sa'ad	originally an airfield near the pumping station on the oil pipeline connecting Kirkuk with Haifa; expanded into an air base and named after an Islamic warrior from ca. 600 AD.
H-3	al-Wallid	originally an airfield near the pumping station on the oil pipeline connecting Kirkuk with Haifa; expanded into an air base and named after the Islamic warrior and leader Khalid Bin al-Wallid from ca. 600 AD
Habbaniya	-	former RAF Habbaniya, not in use as of 1991
Kirkuk	al-Hurrya	constructed by Ottomans in the 1910s; means "liberty" in Arabic
Kut	Abu Ubayda al-Jarrah	newly constructed in the 1970s; named after a religious and military leader from ca. 600 AD
Mosul	Firnas	named after a legendary middle-age Andalusian Arab who attempted to fly using feathered wings
Mudaysis	Talha	forward operating base
Qarayya West	Saddam	newly constructed in the 1970s; named after Iraqi President Saddam Hussein at-Tikriti
Rashid	Rashid	former RAF Hinaidi; not operational since the mid-1980s
Shaiba	Wahda	former RAF Shaiba; means "unity" in Arabic
Tallil	Ali Ibn Abu Talib	newly constructed in the 1970s; named after a religious and military leader from ca. 600 AD
Taqaddum	Tammuz	constructed next to former RAF Habbaniya; named after the Babylonian month of Tammuz (7th month in the year)

afterburners pending a 180-degree turn, thus causing the Americans to lose sight of him.[3]

Well to the east of Anderson was the Tomcat with Alwine and Cloyd, escorting an EA-6B on the central of the three stations facing Baghdad. The crew did notice 'high and fast activity' to the north-west but was tied by the Navy's fighter doctrine of the time: under no condition were they to abandon the Prowler unless it was directly threatened. Alwine explained:

Our task was SEAD. We were in front of everybody else, Prowlers jamming all the way in. We thus "masked" a wall of Hornets that were behind us. When TALD decoys were launched from behind us, Prowlers stopped their jamming enabling Iraqi radars to come on and search for us…In this scenario, there was a 360-degree threat sector around us, thus we remained committed to the Prowler we were escorting…Then HARMs were released….[4]

After making a wide turn, the Iraqi came back for his second attempt: he powered up his Smerch-A2 and, with the help of ground control, acquired a target 38km (20.5nm) ahead of him. When the range was down to 29km (15.6nm), he fired one R-40RD missile and kept his Smerch-A2 locked-on. At 03.50hrs, the hefty Soviet missile detonated beneath the cockpit of the F/A-18C (163484/AA403), piloted by LCDR Scott 'Spike' Speicher, slewing the aircraft 50-60 degrees right, causing it to shear off external fuel tanks and one of its HARMs. The badly injured pilot ejected from the stricken aircraft but died later.[5] Alwine recalled the moment:

We were in a period when our Prowler was not jamming enemy radars and evading some SAMs, when, in a left-hand turn, in the left quarter panel of the windscreen, I saw a huge fireball at about our altitude. I levelled my wings and steadied with the flaming jet in my HUD, then rolled inverted and followed it down until it hit the ground….For a moment, I had lost track of our Prowler at that point, but knew he was nearby on station. As we got back to altitude and station, we rolled over and directly below us was the glow of four cockpit holes of our EA-6B. It was crazy seeing him right there like that… based on my understanding of the geometry of the mission, I thought it was an A-7 that was hit….

Dawoud remained in the combat zone. Indeed, he was now behind the Hornets, deep in the flank of the USN's strike package, but still in front of the next formation: four A-6Es from VA-75. This time, the AWACS reacted on time, calling the Intruder pilots on the

Most of the major IrAF air bases in service as of 1990-1991 were comparable to massive fortifications. Those in central and southern Iraq were constructed by Yugoslav companies in the 1970s and 1980s. They had multiple runways and taxiways that could be used as auxiliary runways, all of their major facilities were constructed underground, and all aircraft parked inside hardened aircraft shelters, each of which with its own power supply. Abu Ubayda al-Jarrah AB, visible in this photograph, was home-base to two Mirage F.1-squadrons. (Photo by Martin Rosenkranz)

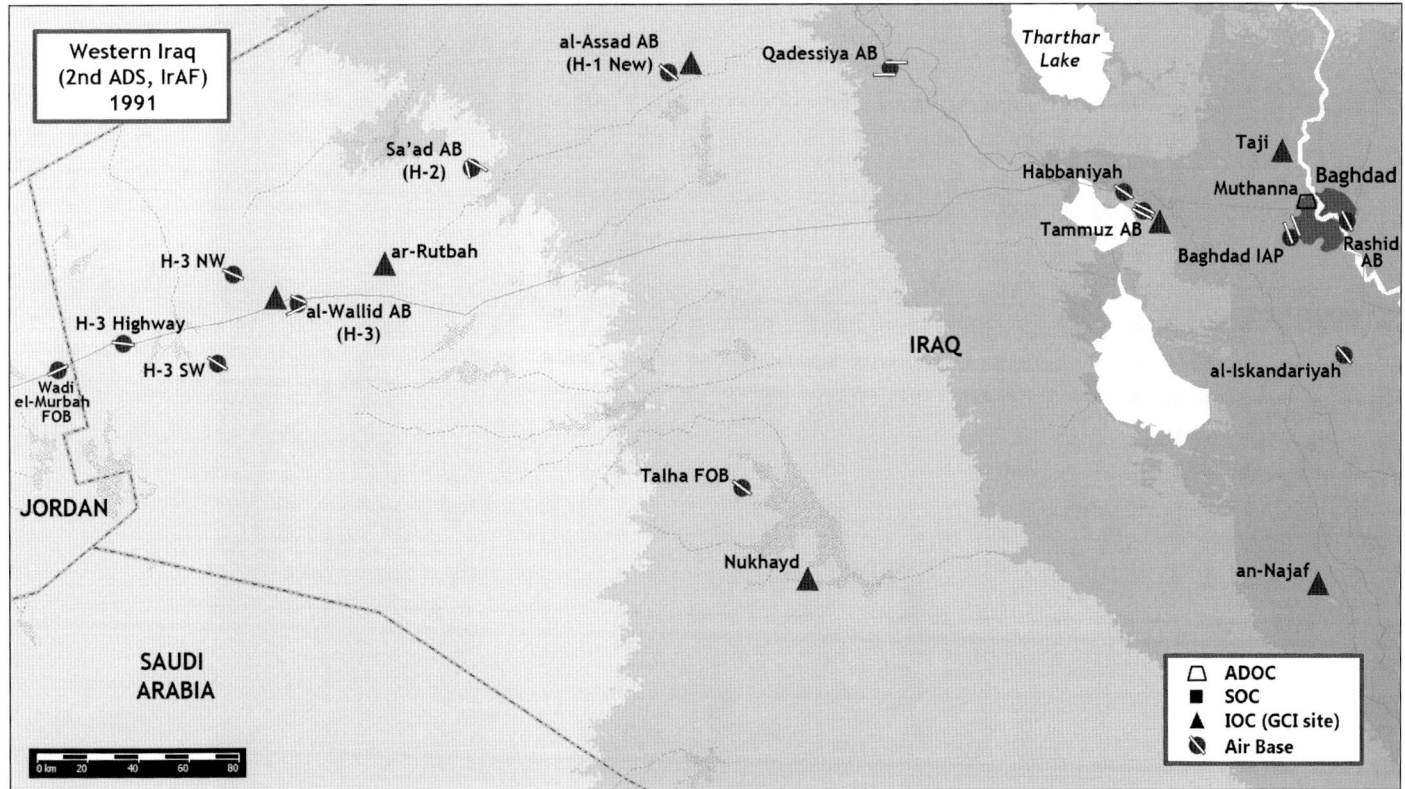

A map of western Iraq, with major air bases of the IrAF as of 1991. This was the area where most of the air combats involving Navy Tomcats took place. (Map by Tom Cooper)

right frequency to issue a warning. Seconds later, the ALR-67 RHAW of the Intruder flown by LCDR Mike 'Ziggy' Steinmetz and CDR Robert Besal lit up to warn them of being tracked by an interceptor. Looking up, the crew saw the big MiG-25 slicing down at them with its afterburners on. Steinmetz broke right, but Dawoud did not even attempt to fire: his ground control ordered him not to because it was concerned he might be targeting one of two MiG-29s that had been in this area about ten minutes earlier. Frustrated, the Iraqi blazed by and up, made another 180-degree turn before starting to re-attack. Although identifying his target positively, Dawoud was once again denied permission to open fire, and ordered back to Tammuz AB: despite problems with his navigation system, and mines sewn by RAF Tornados, he landed safely a few minutes later.[6]

Not aware of the loss even after one of the Hornet pilots reported an airborne explosion at 24,000ft – and that as a 'result of an air-to-air engagement' – Hornets, Corsairs and Intruders proceeded with their mission and delivered an attack that was assessed as having caused heavy damage to the enemy air defences. Alwine concluded:

> We were post-strike tanking when 3 Hornets showed up low on gas. We backed out to let them top off. By the time we got back on the hose, the tanker had to drag us towards his base, away from *Saratoga*, so we were about 30 minutes behind the rest of the package to land. I was later told that the deck crew was told our airwing had lost a jet, but not whose it was. The Sunliners and Be-Devilers were all waiting to see which of us would be the one coming home. It was a sickening feeling when I found out it was Spike that went down.[7]

A BUNCH OF SOFT KILLS

Whether based on sheer reputation of the F-14 or not, the Navy's 'delay and disrupt' fighter doctrine played a crucial role in the next engagement: although resulting in a literal 'bunch of soft kills', but no missile exchanges, it can be said that this turned into a major power demonstration for the Tomcat. The action began when USS *Kennedy* and USS *Saratoga* launched a combined operation to strike the ADOC at Wallid, and bomb Sa'ad AB, early in the morning of 17 January.[8]

The first into the target zone were four F-14As led by CDR Bob 'Sundance' Davis, CO VF-32. Eight additional Tomcats escorted eight A-6Es (some armed with HARMs), four A-7Es and three EA-6Bs. At that point in time, the E-2 controller announced four groups of 'bogeys' – a total of at least 12 Iraqi interceptors airborne – near Sa'ad AB, but did not declare them as enemy, prompting one of the Tomcat pilots into thinking '…who would be CAPping over the bad airfield on day one of the war?'[9]

As the Navy formation crossed the border, Davis's Tomcats acquired the nearest enemy flight – four MiG-29s – with their AWG-9s. By the way the Iraqis flew their orbits, it was clear they were versed in countering F-14s and denying them long-range Phoenix shots. Of course, the ROEs negated that option anyway.

Davis took no chances, though, and his formation spiked the Iraqis with its AWG-9s in PDSTT-mode. The Iraqis reacted promptly: one division headed southwest along a desert highway for H-3, the others turned in the northern and north-eastern directions. The only one to apparently think about engaging the incoming Navy formation was a single MiG-25 pilot that – while underway at 12,192m (40,000ft) and Mach 1.2 – turned right in the direction of one of the approaching EA-6Bs that was meanwhile emitting its jamming. Rather unsurprisingly considering the power of the 'music' emitted by the Prowler, the Iraqi failed to achieve a lock-on and gave up, turning away to follow the others that distanced towards the north. Just to make sure, Davis then split his division and sent two Tomcats after the four MiGs that ran away in the south-western direction. The Tomcats thus won the air battle for H-2 without firing a single shot.

DOCTRINAL APPROACH

Underway as a RIO on F-14A 160397/AC204, piloted by LCDR Drew Brugal, was LCDR Dave 'Hey Joe' Parsons, the overall mission commander for this operation. That and the Tomcat crewed by LT 'Voodoo' Voors and LT 'BUNO' Washington (which suffered a failure of the instrumental navigation system during this mission), flew as HVU-escort: both were thus in the rear of the formation, but following the action ahead of them with help of the fighter-fighter datalink. With Iraqi interceptors out of the way, the strike went well and all of the involved fighter-bombers emerged undamaged for the flight back home. Parsons recalled what happened next:

> …we were doctrinal bound to stay with the Prowlers, not turn away from them. The Prowlers were heading south back to Saudi Arabia when the AWACS started giving us calls that the MiGs that had retired north of target had reversed course and were trying to run us down from behind after strike package had proceeded south…. Topgun preached our primary mission was to "delay and disrupt" attempts by enemy interceptors to target our HVU, not to charge after MiGs and thus expose our assigned HVU. Thus we decided to stay with the Prowlers until they were safely out of the area, or the MiGs got too close, and then to detach the rear two Tomcats to deal with MiGs, leaving the other two to escort the Prowlers…I was telling the Prowlers to 'buster' – accelerate to maximum speed – so we could engage sooner, but they did not

A KC-135 and a KA-6D (tanker-variant of the Intruder, visible third from left is an example from VA-85) seen while refuelling a pair of F-14As (from VF-33), two F/A-18Cs and an EA-6B (from VAQ-137) on the way to Iraq.

A pair of VF-32's Tomcats crossing Saudi Arabia at high altitude underway for a mission to Iraq. Each jet was armed with a pair of AIM-9M Sidewinders, AIM-7M Sparrows and AIM-54C Phoenix missiles, which was a typical warload early during the war. (Photo by CDR David Parsons)

'Gipsy 204' was the radio call-sign of the F-14A crewed by LCDR Brugal and LCDR Parsons on 17 January 1991. (Photo by CDR David Parsons)

Availability of a large number of 'big' tankers – like USAF KC-135s and KC-10As – was crucial for the success of Operation Desert Storm. This photograph shows an F-14A from VF-32 waiting its turn to refuel from the KC-135 in the background. (Photo by CDR David Parsons)

we watched them pass us and launch their Sparrows: both MiGs were downed.[10]

WRONG FREQUENCY

With MiG-29s out of the way, the action moved further west, where four F-14A+s led by the XO of VF-103, CDR Brian 'Rocky' Fitzpatrick (with LCDR Dana Dervay as RIO, on F-14A+ 163215/AA204) were ahead of an even bigger strike package underway across the coast into Saudi Arabia. While still refuelling from USAF KC-135s, the Tomcats were alerted about the presence of MiG-29s, and then three other groups of Iraqi fighters over the target zone.

Fitzpatrick formed his flight into a wall and increased speed while crossing the border to Iraq, heading directly for Wallid AB. About 75km (40nm) short of H-3, the F-14 crews were informed that 'bandits' were leaving the target zone northeast towards H-2. Fitzpatrick did not follow: instead, he continued to follow the plan, leading his formation to the west and then to the north of the heavily protected target zone: around H-3. As they rounded the corner towards the east, their AWG-9s picked up four contacts, 120km (65nm) away, but coming straight at them. All four crews promptly sorted the targets between themselves and prepared to fire. Just at that moment in time, Fitzpatrick was disturbed for a few seconds: he had got a 'spike' on his RHAW gear, from his left rear: an enemy aircraft had locked its radar on him and was taking aim. Although concerned, he decided to press forward in an eastern direction, popping chaff and manoeuvring hard while his wingman was checking his rear. Since no attack came from the western direction, the Tomcats continued in the eastern: their crews planning to fire two Phoenix missiles at each bandit. At that point in time, it became crucial to obtain a positive identification of enemy aircraft from the AWACS. However, even as the F-14s approached to less than 37km (20nm), the E-2C was not responding. Left without

hear us because of the power of the jamming they emitted….. We were about to cross-turn and engage them, when I detected two F-15s coming north on a reverse heading, out of Saudi Arabia, already supersonic and obviously vectored onto the MiGs. So,

PROWLER TROUBLE

While many assessments about what specific aircraft types can or cannot do are based on experiences from realistic exercises, there are always crucial areas of performance that can never be 'tested' in peace. One of these was the full power and capabilities of the 'music' – electronic warfare emissions – deployed by aircraft like the Grumman EA-6B Prowler.

The Prowler was a result of efforts to integrate electronic warfare aircraft into the carrier airwing. The original variant, EA-6A, was developed during the Vietnam War, and comprised a converted Grumman A-6A Intruder two-seat bomber, fitted with more than 30 different antennae for monitoring, classifying, recording, jamming and deceiving enemy radar transmissions. The EA-6B Prowler appeared towards the end of the same conflict and was a major step forward. It included a stretched fuselage with a cockpit for four crewmembers: pilot, ECM-officer (who managed navigation, communications, defensive ECM and the dispensing of chaff), and two electronic warfare operators (EWOs). The Prowler came together with much improved and more powerful equipment centred on up to five ALQ-99 high-power tactical jamming pods. While one of these was installed in an aerodynamic shape atop the fin, the other four were carried underwing and included windmill generators to supply their power requirements.

As of 1990-1991, the USN had one electronic warfare squadron of four EA-6Bs for each of its CVWs. However, their crews were prohibited from deploying the full power of ALQ-99 during peacetime exercises. Thus, the first time they went into a war – against Iraq, on 17 January 1991 – some of their potential took everybody by surprise. It turned out that when 'cut loose', the Prowlers caused the RHAW gear of F-14s to literally go crazy, and jammed not only their own IFF-signals, but also much of the radio communications. Indeed, a subsequent investigation revealed that their emissions were one of the principal reasons for communication problems experienced by multiple Navy formations underway over Iraq on the first day of the war.

An EA-6B Prowler of VAQ-130 Zappers seen in January 1991, when the unit was operating as part of CVW-3 from USS *John F Kennedy* (CV-67). Rather unexpectedly, Tomcats flying HVU-escort for Prowlers were to see much action during Operation Desert Storm. (Photo by CDR David Parsons)

choice, Fitzpatrick decided to obtain positive identification with help of the TCS. Obviously, this required all four F-14s to switch their AWG-9s from the TWS into the PDSTT-mode and, as could be expected, that provoked instantaneous reaction from the Iraqis: as soon as they were 'spiked' by the Tomcats' radars, they promptly broke hard north and dived to minimal altitude, running away. A life-time opportunity was lost due to a communication problem.[11]

As the Tomcats now started to chase the north-bound Iraqis, the E-2 suddenly came up to report two bandits to the south: whether these scrambled from Wallid AB, or belonged to the formation scared when spiked by F-14s flying a sweep towards Sa'ad AB, minutes earlier, is unclear. What is certain is that this meant there were Iraqi interceptors between the F-14s and the strike formation of 40 jets Fitzpatrick was supposed to protect: moreover, the new pair of Iraqi interceptors was a threat, while the others were running away! Left without a choice, Fitzpatrick ordered his formation back south.[12]

MIG-21s AGAINST THE WALL
Before the four Tomcats could get back, the two Iraqi jets detected by the E-2 – both were MiG-21bis from No. 47 Squadron, flown by 1st Lieutenant Abbas Khudair and 1st Lieutenant Laith Laeeth – accelerated to supersonic and turned south: straight into a 'wall' of Hornets! Facing them from west towards east were LT Nick 'Mongo' Mongillo with CDR William 'Maggot' McKee (XO of VFA-81). About a mile apart to their right were LCDR Mark 'MRT' Fox, and LCDR Chuck 'Bouncer' Osborne (VFA-83).[13] This time it was the E-2 controller that attempted to raise the Hornets on the

A 'MiG-sweep' division of F-14A+s from VF-103 (foreground) and VF-74 seen high above Saudi Arabia while underway to Iraq. (Photo by CDR David Parsons)

A TCS-view of a KC-135 tanker of the USAF, seen from on the TID in the rear cockpit of an F-14A from VF-41 in 1991. Meant to enable visual target identification from dozens of miles away, the AXX-1 proved a mixed blessing during the Second Persian Gulf War.

radio: however, because he was using the USAF-style codenames for H-3 ('Manny'), the pilots were preoccupied with setting up the decisive phase of their first mission of the war, and thinking the calls were for Fitzpatrick's Tomcat formation further north, the F/A-18C-fliers overheard everything. It was only once the E-2 controller called McKee's mission call sign and informed him the bandits were on his nose, just 27km (15nm) away, that there was a reaction. Even then, neither McKee nor Osborne had heard the 'bandit' call, but Fox and Mongillo did. While McKee attempted to visually identify the two approaching jets, the other two pilots quickly switched to air-to-air, acquired the approaching enemy and ran electronic identification. Certain he had heard the call 'bandit' from the E-2C controller, and that thus all the ROEs had been satisfied, Fox fired an AIM-9M Sidewinder at the leading MiG-21. Because the missile was smokeless, he lost sight of it. Uncertain about the result, he promptly set up an AIM-7M Sparrow shot and fired again. A few seconds later his first missile found its mark, exploding the MiG in a bright flash: the Sparrow then followed, impacting the burning wreckage. A similar engagement followed on the western side of the formation: satisfied he was following all the ROEs, Mongillo fired a Sparrow as his target was only 4.63km (2.5nm) away. The missile pulled to the right as soon as it came off the rail, but then corrected itself and went for a direct hit that disintegrated the MiG-21. Both of the two young pilots from No. 47 Squadron were killed.[14]

No sooner were the two MiG-21s shot down – just three miles south-west of Wallid – when the E-2C controller announced four additional bandits rising from H-3. Climbing to 7,010m (23,000ft), this formation of MiG-29s first went 'hot' – nose-on – on the Hornets, well inside Sparrow range, before realising their mistake and turning hard, diving towards the east directly over the Iraqi base. Having no positive identification this time, all four F/A-18C pilots held their fire. Now almost over their target, they decided not to pursue and all switched back to air-to-ground mode and bombed instead. Certainly enough, Fitzpatrick's formation was coming down from the north: it was only 28km (15nm) away when the two MiG-21s were shot down. However, it was now short on fuel and, with Hornets dive-bombing, HARMs and SAMs flying around, the Tomcats decided to follow their doctrine and cover the bombers as these withdrew towards the Saudi border.

RADIO DISCIPLINE

Still having problems communicating with the E-2C, Fitzpatrick switched to the USAF E-3 frequency – only to find out that his formation had two bandits on its tail, approximately 37km (20nm) to the rear. This was a pair of MiG-21s from No. 47 Squadron scrambled early and sent north-westwards: the leader of the pair was the one who spiked Fitzpatrick's Tomcat earlier. The two Iraqis had been after the four F-14s ever since. Low on fuel, Fitzpatrick – reluctantly – decided not to engage; instead, he passed the target info on to a pair of F-14s from VF-74. The Tomcats in question were crewed by CDR Charles 'Cuddles' Wyatt (XO VF-74), with LTJG Craig 'Pep' Peppe in the rear (on F-14A+ 162919/AA101), and LT Mike 'Buick' Eberhardt, with LCDR Scott 'Stewie' Stewart as RIO. Wyatt explained:

> … the mission was to protect an EA-6B Prowler providing jamming support for four Hornets tasked with bombing H-3 in western Iraq….The launch of *Saratoga* did not go well. We lost the entire system off the catapult shot: had no radar, no inertial navigation system … nothing. Essentially, the mighty jet was a supersonic twin-engine Cessna with a 20mm gun now. Our airwing strike protocols at the time were to return overhead and recover aboard ship after launch of the strike group was complete, and have a spare launched to take our place, but that wasn't going to happen. No way was I going to miss this battle. I've had over 3,000 hours in the jet and had experience in getting the system back. Another part of the airwing strike protocols was for aircraft to proceed individually after the launch and rendezvous on the tankers over Saudi Arabia, about 200nm from our ship in the Red

Sea. So, Pep and I proceeded eastbound using the wet compass and the desert to navigate to where we thought the tanker package would be. Of course, there were no communications on any frequency to give away the impeding strike [to the Iraqis]. We found the tankers, but during the rendezvous I noticed these aircraft were from USS America and their strike was to attack H-2 air base about five minutes prior to our strike on H-3. Knowing my group was on tanker track about 100 miles to the west, we proceeded in that direction and eventually found them.[15]

As Wyatt pressed on, Peppe diligently worked full time to recover the AWG-9. Eventually, Wyatt and Peppe found the 'right ' tankers:

> During the rendezvous on the tankers, with 20 plus fighters and bombers joining with no communications, we did many belly-checks to prevent collisions, which forces your bearing line for rendezvous aft of normal. To correct, one pulls hard back to achieve the proper bearing line. During those manoeuvres, pulling 4-5gs, I would select Pilot Lock-on Mode on the AWG-9, which forced the radar into a narrow rapid scan movement. Under increased g-forces, if the radar would ever wake up, that was the time. Don't ask me why that worked; it wasn't in books anywhere, just something I stumbled upon during my time on the aircraft. It just did: the radar responded. We regained a degraded radar mode: it was usable for the mission, even if not optimum. We joined the tanker, refuelled, joined our wingman and the Prowler, and pushed in country.

The situation remained quiet until the strike package approached the target zone, and the supporting aircraft began releasing TALDs. That is when the Iraqis reacted by activating their radars and scrambling their interceptors. Wyatt heard the Hornets identifying two enemy aircraft and then shooting them down. Shortly after:

> ...Pep got two contacts in the north-western corner of Iraq, near the Syrian border, range 35nm, hot. He asked the E-2 to declare their identity: the – delayed – response was, "friendly". Around that time, one of the Hornets that was shooting TALDs passed by in southern direction. His Mode IV IFF was malfunctioning and for the next 5-7 minutes it seemed he was broadcasting his position, speed, and altitude on the strike-frequency about every 30 seconds (had I known where he was, I would have shot his ass down myself, just to shut him up). Needless to say, the strike frequency was already clobbered with tactical stuff and MiGs flying everywhere, the bombers egressing south, and our situational awareness had degraded to zero. Unknown to me at the time, Rocky's division MiG-sweep was being pursued by MiGs about 20 miles behind him and he was still well away from exiting Iraq. He tried, numerous times, and unsuccessfully, to reach me for help, but we had them on fighter-fighter datalink and knew exactly where his flight was located. The reasons for not hearing him were two-fold: first the IFF-sour Hornet, second the situational reports by others, and thirdly our impeding merge with the unknown contacts that were not at 20nm, not. Pep had broken lock on and checked north instead, but Stewie still had them locked up. Unfortunately, his TCS was non-operational. Mine was good but Pep couldn't re-gain the lock on due to the degraded radar. We scrammed the Prowler, and [LCDR Jim] 'Panic' [Panigall] did as I had taught him on numerous briefs. He flew a split-S to the deck, as fast and as low as he could until feeling there is no threat. By now, the MiG-21s approached to 11 miles, but then beamed north. Since Stewie had a lock-down mode on his radar, and mine was non-operational, I passed lead to Buick. We headed north for two minutes, until reaching an area said to be protected by an I-HAWK SAM site – which was a bad ass mack daddy of the SAMs inside 20 miles or so. I spent at least a minute screaming at Buick to head south until he responded and executed, and all the time Rocky was asking for help chasing him, but I never heard him.

Through all of this, it appeared that there was no reaction from the E-2: later on, it turned out the controller's 'friendly' was meant for somebody else but issued on the wrong frequency. In turn, while certain the two jets in front of him were enemy, Wyatt followed the ROEs and did not open fire. Eberhardt and Stewart's AWG-9 must have spiked the Iraqis, forcing them to break and fly the 'beaming' manoeuvre: to turn perpendicular to the Tomcats and disappear in the doppler notch of their AWG-9s. Eventually, the two F-14s turned back south:

> We headed out of country for the tanker. Some 5-7 minutes after we had scrammed the Prowler, already after crossing the border to Saudi Arabia, Panic called me on the fighter frequency, "Cuds, Panic.... Am I cleared to

A row of VF-74 F-14A+s seen neatly parked next to the bridge of USS *Saratoga*, during Operation Desert Storm. Visible in the background is one of VAW-125's E-2Cs.

The F-14A+ (then F-14B) 162919/AA101, flown by Wyatt and Peppe on 17 January 1991, seen about a year later.

A view of the TID in the rear cockpit of an F-14A during a left turn, with the AWG-9 in the TWS-mode and tracking a target about 20nm away - roughly similar to what Metcalfe could see during the engagement with an Iraqi MiG-25 on the evening of 17 January 1991.

climb?" OMG! I started laughing my rear off! Told him, "Roger" or something like that, so he wouldn't hear me laughing.

Ultimately, the discipline of multiple F-14 and F/A-18 crews, inducted through years of thorough training, saved the IrAF from suffering massive losses over Wallid AB that day. Even if both of the downed MiG-21 pilots were killed, this was still a very limited price in comparison to what could have happened had only one of the Navy's section or division commanders decided to violate the ROEs. In turn, the thesis was proven beyond any doubt, that the Iraqis would be extremely reluctant to directly confront any of the USN's F-14s.

SPARROW AGAINST FOXBAT

The USS *Saratoga* and the USS *Kennedy* launched their third strike on Iraq during the evening of 17 January 1991. This time, four A-6Es from VA-35 were to deploy Mk.83 bombs for a multi-axis, low-altitude attack on the fuel storage depot of Wallid AB, while another Intruder formation was to bomb Sa'ad AB. They were protected by two EA-6Bs armed with HARMs, which in turn were escorted by two F-14A+s. A section of Tomcats from VF-103 was tasked with a MiG-sweep ahead of the strike package, and their crews were briefed that while USAF F-15s would be flying a CAP along the border, once inside Iraq, there would be no friendly aircraft in front of them.[16]

The mission launched in good order: problems emerged once the formation reached the Saudi coast. Dense clouds and severe turbulence at the IFR-point forced the USAF KC-135s to start refuelling Navy aircraft below the overcast, and then 'tow' them up through the overcast to the smoother air above. This passage through the clouds was by no means easy: not only could one of VF-103's two Tomcats not complete its IFR-operation and was forced to abort, but turbulence was so heavy that all of the strike package from USS *Kennedy* was forced to turn back. This left the other Tomcat crew tasked with the sweep – pilot LT Tim 'Glaze' Glaser and his RIO LT Alan 'Radar' Metcalfe (flying F-14A+ 161440/AA207) – facing a choice of aborting or continuing the mission. Not being of the kind to leave the bombers alone, Glaser pressed on as a single-aircraft sweep.

Once off the tanker, the lonesome Tomcat passed the two F-15Cs CAPping at the border and proceeded north heading for ar-Rutbah, about 55.5km (30nm) ahead of A-6s: because his ALR-67 RHAW failed, Glaser constantly rolled left and right to check the skies below and behind him. After passing Rutbah, the crew saw massive fireworks lighting the night to their left, as the air defences of Wallid opened fire: concluding they were outside the envelope of the local SAM sites, Glaser and Metcalfe decided to continue on a northern course for a few seconds longer, before heading west and passing north of the Iraqi air base.

Unknown to the Tomcat crew, by that time the IrAF had one interceptor approaching the combat zone: a MiG-25PDS that scrambled from Tammuz AB with the order to head west – approximately in same direction where a night before two other Foxbats clashed with USAF EF-111As and F-15Es, and then with Navy fighter-bombers. This time, the Iraqi continued further west: intending to attempt a different approach and, instead of cruising at medium altitude, the Foxbat flew all the way to Wallid AB at low altitude. This and the fact that the MiG-25's flight path was beaming (flying perpendicular to) the AWACS call-sign Yukon, resulted in it remaining undetected until reaching H-3: it was only once the USN strike package approached its target that the jet was ordered to accelerate to supersonic speed and climb to an altitude of 6,000m (19,685ft).[17]

Scanning the skies in front of them with the AWG-9 in TWS mode, Glaser and Metcalfe meanwhile reached a point north-east of H-3. Underway at 9,144m (30,000ft), they initiated their planned left turn: only a second later, their radar registered a contact bearing 312 degrees, 81km (44nm) away. The E-2 controller in charge of

Far too few details about Iraqi MiG-25 operations in 1991 have become known over the last 30 years because former members of the Foxbat community are forced to hide due to a manhunt by the IRGC. This photograph shows Colonel Saleh Maheed al-Jabouri with the MiG-25PD serial number 25205 inside a hardened aircraft shelter at Taqaddum AB in 1990. Notable is a single R-40TD on the inboard underwing pylon and the huge, 5,000-litre drop tank under the centreline (nick-named 'dinghy' by the Iraqis). (via Ali Tobchi)

the mission never responded to any of their calls: instead, Yukon requested their position off 'Manny' – the call-sign for H-3. Metcalfe misunderstood the message and never made a bullseye call, but as the closure rate to the contact ahead of them was at least 1,000 knots (1,852km/h!), Glaser had no doubt about its identity. When the range decreased to 37km (20nm), he switched to Sparrow and asked Metcalfe to lock the contact, intending to fire and then execute the F-pole manoeuvre: essentially, to dive to the side while keeping his target spiked by the AWG-9. The RIO achieved a lock-on, and the pilot took a zero-aspect AIM-7M shot from a range of 24km (13nm), before cranking left, as his target was at 5,000m (16,404ft) and climbing, meanwhile about 65km (35nm) north of the nearest A-6E.

At that moment, Metcalfe called out 'Fox-3' on the radio: this was a call-sign for firing an AIM-54 Phoenix missile. Quickly realising his mistake, he corrected himself and called 'Fox-1' (a call-sign for an AIM-7), but the damage was already done: the Fox-3 call sent everybody on board the E-2 and E-3 into a frenzy due to the relatively unknown capability of the Phoenix and the general confusion, further enhanced by the Hawkeye's failure to reply to Glaser's and Metcalfe's calls, and Yukon mistaking Glaser's F-14 for one of the Tomcats flying HVU-escort! At the same time Metcalfe corrected his call, the E-2 controller called one of the A-6s a 'bandit' at '215 and 9 off Manny'. Unsurprisingly, Yukon reacted with, 'That's a friendly!' The E-2 ignored and repeated the call misidentifying an A-6 as a 'bandit', now at '212 and 8 off Manny'. Unsurprisingly, the AWACS once again corrected with, 'That's a friendly! ...Yukon shows 2 friendlies south [of] Manny, 10 miles tracking north-east!'. Actually, by now nobody knew where Glaser's F-14A+ was, nor where it was heading or at whom was it firing: therefore, the AWACS ordered a cease-fire. Not correlating the calls, Metcalfe promptly shut down the AWG-9, thus – at least in theory – terminating the guidance of the AIM-7M. With his displays turning blank, Glaser wrenched the Tomcat to the left, and after checking his six for threats redirected his attention low and to his left, towards Wallid AB, as the time was approaching for the A-6s to hit their target.

Deep down below, the first A-6E zig-zagged between the heavy anti-aircraft fire to release its six Mk.83s with unknown results. The second Intruder (161668/AA510) was narrowly missed by one SAM, and then the crew saw another approaching from its two o'clock position. The pilot dispensed chaff and made a hard turn but it was too late: the missile detonated closely behind the aircraft, setting an engine on fire. With the A-6E out of control, Lieutenants Robert Wetzel and Jeffrey Zaun had no other option left but to eject. Unable to get into the correct physical position before activating their escape system, both were wounded before hitting the ground only one mile outside Wallid AB. Zaun then found his badly injured pilot and decided to stay with him, instead of escaping over the nearby border to Jordan. The third A-6 was forced into such violent manoeuvres, that it missed the target by more than a mile. The fourth A-6E (158539/AA502) then received a hit by another Roland SAM, which forced the crew to jettison its ordnance off-target and divert to al-Jawf airport in Saudi Arabia. Although landing safely, this Intruder was subsequently written off.[18]

Now passing close by Wallid AB in a south-western direction, Glaser's Tomcat was then fired upon by at least three SA-6s, but the pilot managed to evade by executing two hard break turns and then unloading accelerating to Mach 1.4. On the way back to Saudi Arabia, the crew experienced difficulties while trying to refuel from a KC-135, and thus diverted to al-Jawf. After refuelling, Glaser and Metcalfe returned to the USS *Saratoga*, to become the final jet back from that fateful mission. During their debrief on the carrier they were accused of shooting down the Intruder flown by Wetzel and Zaun and subjected to a detailed investigation that went on for days. Ultimately, the crew was cleared of any wrongdoing and resumed combat operations over Iraq.[19]

What happened with the Iraqi MiG-25 and the AIM-7M fired by Glaser remains unknown to this day. The few Iraqi Foxbat pilots that survived all that befell their homeland have been in hiding ever since, and refuse to speak out. Even so, it remains unclear what they might know. Another important person that might have some answers, the contemporary commander of Wallid AB, has refused to provide an interview. What is certain is that a detailed review of Glaser's engagement revealed that the AIM-7M was airborne for approximately 20 seconds – more than enough time to hit the target. It is nearly certain that this was also the case: however, if the Foxbat was shot down, it crashed in the Akashat area – one of the emptiest and most inhospitable corners of Iraq, in recent years brimming with the activity of the notorious 'Islamic State'...

FRUSTRATING DOCTRINE

While the CAOC continued pummelling the Iraqi air defences with additional airstrikes all through 18 January 1991, the IrAF took a 'break' to study its early experiences and re-assess its options.

ROLAND AT H-3[20]

Because Iraq was originally preparing for a war with Israel before invading Kuwait, and because Wallid AB was the closest IrAF air base to its potential opponent, the Iraqis took care to significantly bolster the local air defences. As of 1990-1991, the air base was actually a complex of one major airfield and three dispersal sites, capable of housing two complete wings of fighter bombers. Unsurprisingly, the area was protected by a full brigade of SA-6 SAMs, including three SAM sites, each of which was reinforced by a single Roland-2 firing unit. Close-in air defence of the complex and the SAM sites consisted of a full anti-aircraft regiment with four batteries equipped with automatic, radar-guided 37mm and 57mm guns.

The commander of one of the Roland-2 firing units protecting Wallid/H-3 AB on the evening of 17 January 1991 was 1st Lieutenant Rabe'e, an officer that already had a Northrop F-5E Tiger II of the IRIAF to his credit from the previous war. His TEL was deployed about five kilometres away from the SA-6 SAM site he was protecting. Although the incoming US airstrike was announced by the 2nd SOC quite early, nothing was happening, and thus Rabe'e initially kept the radar of his system on standby, before deciding to go outside to take a look. The night was pitch black and the desert cold: only a few dimmed lights emanated from the nearby SA-6 site. As he was returning to his command module, Rabe'e saw a brilliant ball of flame from the same direction: a call to the HQ of the SA-6 site revealed that its commander was killed by a direct hit on the fire-control radar, obviously from an AGM-88 HARM. Alerted, but cautious, Rabe'e decided to wait patiently and keep his radar on standby until a more opportune moment: indeed, he waited until the 2nd SOC informed him that enemy aircraft were within 20km. After powering his fire-control radar up, Rabe'e quickly selected the nearest target and ordered his crew to engage. The fire-control officer pressed the launch button once, then a few seconds later, again: after hearing the distinctive roar of two Roland missiles leaving their tubes, the crew heard a dull detonation, while their radar screen showed the signal of a hit. About an hour after the US strike, the HQ 2nd ADS then called to congratulate: an A-6 Intruder had been shot down and its crew had been captured.[21]

As delivered to Iraq, the Roland-2 was a command link guided point defence SAM system. Every firing unit mounted a complete acquisition and fire-control equipment on the chassis of the MAN-truck-mounted 'shelter' (100 units acquired by Iraq) or AMX-30 tank (13 units): the system proved highly resistant to jamming, thanks to deployment of the monopulse angular tracking technique. Two Roland-2 firing units were responsible for the loss of one of VA-35's A-6E, and the write-off of another, late on 17 January 1991. The example shown here belonged to the French Army. (Photo by Olivier Carneau)

Several conclusions were obvious: one was that the Kari IADS and ATMS was badly damaged and dozens of radars had been knocked out. However, the principal command and control networks of the 1st and 2nd ADS, and most of the SAM sites were still intact. Another conclusion was that the IrAF had to stop scrambling its interceptors to face ingressing enemy airstrikes on a case-by-case basis, and to stop flying CAPs: instead, it was to conduct only well-prepared operations, deploying pairs of MiG-25s, MiG-29s, or Mirage F.1s for hit-and-run intercepts on carefully selected targets. These new tactical methods were applied from 19 January – with mixed results.[22]

With USS *Kennedy* and USS *Saratoga* flying all of the Navy's operations from the Red Sea during the first 48 hours of Operation Desert Storm, on 19 January 1991 it was the turn on CVW-1 aboard USS *America* to launch its first major operation. Undertaken in cooperation with CVW-3 embarked aboard *Kennedy*, this saw 12 F/A-18C Hornets from VFA-82 and VFA-86 and 8 A-7Es from VA-46 and VA-72 attacking munitions plants in al-Iskandariyah and Qa Qaa, and a rocket testing facility outside Musayyib. The strike package was protected by five HARM-toting A-7Es and three EA-6Bs from VAQ-137, escorted by four F-14As from VF-32. The attack developed successfully until the involved aircraft faced a strong headwind on the way back to Saudi Arabia – and then came under attack by four MiG-29s from No. 39 Squadron from Qadessiya AB, and two MiG-25s from No. 97 Squadron's detachment forward deployed to Wallid AB the previous day. The Fulcrum-pair led by Captain Jameel Sayhood was delayed: shortly after taking-off from Qadessiya AB, it reported running into four RAF Tornados underway at low altitude, and downing one (no such loss by the Coalition is recorded). Meanwhile, the ground control managed to coordinate an attack by the other Fulcrum-pair, led by Major Sayd, and a pair of MiG-25s led by Captain Neheme, against the rearmost A-7E, piloted by LCDR Val 'VD' Diers, escorted by two F-14As. Once again, the Tomcat pilots followed the Topgun doctrine to the last dot and comma. Thus, while starting their pursuit a full 100km (54nm) behind, Sayd's MiG-29s came dangerously close, as recalled by Diers:

> The Tomcats stayed on each shoulder doing the fighter weave, and I, in frustration, was about to turn solo to engage. I was ready to 'pickle' my drop tank, so to engage with [Side]Winder and guns because they had me cold. There was nothing else I could do. The AWACS female controller – I can still hear her today – said, "You have to do something, they're right there!"[23]

Of course, the AWACS with call-sign 'Cougar' did not stand idle: it vectored multiple formations of USAF F-15C to the scene: arriving 'just in time', these forced the Fulcrums away, and then – despite excellent performance by the Iraqi Foxbat pilots – shot down both MiG-25s.[24]

HARD-LUCK CARRIER

The loss of two precious MiG-25s to USAF F-15s on 19 January prompted the IrAF into another revision of tactics. Realising they were repeatedly decoyed into fighting F-15s, and that their Mirages and MiG-23s were compromised to the enemy and thus nearly worthless, the Iraqis decided to limit their operations to two modes: dedicated anti-F-15 interceptions, and pincer-attacks by single Foxbats and Fulcrums on carefully selected targets. Whenever under threat, pilots were advised to break and head for the nearest concentration of SAM sites. Ironically, this resulted in several additional clashes with F-14s.[25]

The first to experience the new Iraqi tactics was CVW-17, the airwing embarked on USS *Saratoga*, and which at the time was losing more jets than anybody else – partially because its bombers were striking from low altitudes, and partially for no other reason than bad luck. Following a rare intervention by superior officers, the wing changed its tactics to medium-altitude operations: meanwhile it was obvious that the F-14s and SEAD-support could handle the Iraqi interceptors and medium and high-altitude SAM-threats, respectively. Although some still expected this to cause prohibitively high losses, the decision proved to be correct – at least for A-6Es and F/A-18s. Early on 21 January 1991, CVW-17 launched an airstrike on Qadessiya AB, with Intruders from VA-35 this time armed with delayed-action bombs (nick-named 'destructors'), supposed to be deployed from medium altitude. The A-6Es were protected by four F/A-18Cs armed with HARMs and TALDs and two EA-6Bs from VAQ-132 (each of which was armed with one HARM): a pair of F-14A+s from VF-74 flew the MiG-sweep ahead of the attack formation, and each of the Prowlers had its own HVU-escort in the form of one Tomcat from VF-103. The formation did experience some problems with turbulence while refuelling from KC-135s over north-western Saudi Arabia, but all jets completed this operation successfully and moved north on time.

62nd MISSILE BATTERY

The approach of CVW-17's formation was detected by the Soviet-made SPN-30 ECM-system of Unit 128 – a specialised electronic warfare outfit of the IrAF – as VF-74's sweep was crossing the border to Iraq, from nearly 340km (184nm) away.[26] Thus, the Iraqis were left with 22 minutes of time to prepare: their plan was to busy the enemy with SAMs, and then simultaneously hit them with a MiG-29 from No. 39 Squadron and a MiG-25 from No. 96 Squadron.

An Iraqi SA-2 SAM captured by US troops in Kuwait in 1991.

Moreover, the 1st ADS put on alert all the air defence units within its area of responsibility. Primary amongst these was the 146th Missile Brigade, a massive formation responsible for the defence of Tammuz AB and comprising seven SAM sites: three operating S-75M3 Volga (ASCC/NATO-codename 'SA-2E Guideline'), and four operating S-125 Pechora (ASCC/NATO-codename 'SA-3 Goa') missiles. Commanded by Major Saleh, the 62nd Missile Battery was one of the SA-2-equipped elements of the 146th Missile Brigade: although its equipment was old – acquired from the USSR back in 1975 – its crews were relatively young, and possessed little combat experience because Tammuz was rarely attacked by the IRIAF during the Iran-Iraq War. Nevertheless, Saleh took good care to inform himself about all of the experiences of other SAM sites assigned to the 1st and 2nd SOC: correspondingly, he kept his P-12 acquisition/early warning radar and RSN-75V fire-control radar (ASCC/NATO-codenames 'Spoon Rest' and 'Fan Song', respectively) on standby, patiently waiting for his opportunity.[27]

The ill-fated Clubleaf 212 – the F-14A+ BuNo 161430, Modex AA212, seen short of a catapult launch from USS *Saratoga*. (Photo by AA Tony Woodfin, VFA-83)

LOSS OF CLUBLEAF 212

What exactly happened when all of these aircraft met in the skies in between Qadessiya and Tammuz AB is not entirely clear: what is certain is that it remains a sore subject for most of the Navy's Tomcat community until this very day.

A cross-examination of published US sources and available Iraqi sources reveals that one of the two Prowlers took up a station about 60km (32nm) north-west of Tammuz AB. That jet was piloted by LCDR Jim 'Panic' Panigall, with LCDR Mark Nold in the right seat. Their HVU-escort was an F-14A+ (161430/AA212) crewed by LT Devon 'Boots' Jones and LT Larry 'Rat' Slade, and the two jets flew a left-hand racetrack pattern at altitudes between 7,925 and 9,144m (26,000-30,000ft). The sky was still pitch black: the strike was scheduled to hit the target at 06.10hrs local time, about an hour before dawn, and there was a completely solid cloud deck below. As far as US accounts go, no SAM-related signals were registered during the formation's approach to the target zone other than emissions from a Soviet-made P-37 radar (ASCC/NATO-codename Bar Lock): this emitted from the vicinity of Qadessiya AB, and was obviously used for ground control.[28]

When Saleh activated his P-12 for the first time, this detected two targets about 80km away in a south-western direction. Shortly after, a 10 degree sector in the middle of his display turned white: his system was jammed by an EA-6B Prowler. Deciding to wait for the targets to get closer, the Iraqi commander ordered his crew to set the P-12 to standby and cease emitting. About a minute later, he decided to take another look: this time the radar detected two targets at a range of 60km. Before switching off once again, Saleh took care to slew the Fan Song to the P-12: in this fashion, both were aligned in azimuth, enabling faster fire-action. Once both radars were on standby, he ordered his crew to operate the Fan Song in receiver mode only, to check for possible electronic countermeasures: there were none. Meanwhile, the ground control at Qadessiya AB scrambled a MiG-29 from No. 39 Squadron piloted by Lieutenant-Colonel Nabil, and a MiG-25PDS piloted by Major Ibrahim from Tammuz AB.[29]

Before Saleh ordered his crew to power up the Fan Song, he reminded everybody that they were going to measure the range with the help of radar, but then guide their missiles in 'optical mode', with help of a TV camera – and then only if the target was within the engagement envelope of 37km (20nm). Once the radar was online, a single target appeared on the azimuth screen, but was absent from the elevation screen: Saleh quickly moved the wheel that controlled the Fan Song's elevation and, seconds later, the target appeared on this display too. The Iraqi commander noticed that the target was now flying a right-hand turn, at an altitude of 10,000m (32,808ft): he pointed his TV camera unit at the target and, after turning off his Fan Song again, 12 seconds later, three hefty D20 missiles were ripple fired. As these approached their target, Saleh noticed that it accelerated and attempted a hard turn. The first and second missiles missed, but the third detonated underneath it.[30]

The first sign of trouble for Jones and Slade was the sight of a SAM coming up through the clouds: underway in a left turn, Jones added power, then rolled inverted while tightening the break. The missile continued tracking, nevertheless, and detonated in a bright, white flash below and behind the aircraft. The Tomcat shuddered and rolled to the right and then slid into an unrecoverable flat spin, so vicious that the crew was pinned against the front of their cockpits and could not reach the ejection handles. Eventually, Slade managed to grab the handles as they were down to about 3,109m (10,200ft): the crew punched out. After injuring his back on landing under a parachute, the RIO was captured by the Iraqi Army troops later in the morning; Jones evaded and was recovered by a USAF combat search and rescue team including two Fairchild A-10A Thunderbolt

II fighter-bombers and a pair of Sikorsky MH-53J Pave Low III helicopters, eight hours after being shot down.[31]

A LARGE, TWIN-TAILED JET ...
Panigall's crew was about to fire a HARM at the Bar Lock, when Nold saw a missile streaking *horizontally* towards the escorting Tomcat, which was about 1,000 yards abeam and to the right of them. He did not have the time to radio a warning before the 'Tomcat exploded'. Forgetting about the HARM-shoot, Panigall reefed the Prowler into a right-hand turn, watching the downed jet disappear into the clouds below. Then he and his crew saw two flashes, apparently indicating ejection of the crew. Just about that time, one of the two electronic warfare officers in the rear reported another aircraft above and behind them: Panigall and Nold looked in that direction and were startled to sight a large, twin-tailed jet approaching them before activating what appeared to be the largest afterburners ever, and accelerating away in a northern direction. Realising they were deep over Iraq and their escort was shot down, Panigall wasted no time: he pointed the nose down and pushed throttles as far as they would go. The Prowler exceeded its Mach 0.86 speed limit while diving. Once at low altitude, he reported to the AWACS what had happened, stressing there were MiGs in the area – something nobody on the US side was aware of up to that moment. Eventually, the lonesome EA-6B made it safely back to *Saratoga*.[32]

DOGFIGHT WITH FOXBAT
The action south of Assad AB was anything but over. Because the ground control was late in ordering him to power up his Smerch-A2, Ibrahim found himself too close behind the target to engage with any of his four R-40s. However, Nabil was behind him and in a perfect position to attack: the Foxbat pilot thus broke away, making space for Nabil's R-27R to hit the F-14. The MiG-29 pilot disengaged and – after claiming to have shot down a TLAM on the way back to his base – landed safely. Ibrahim remained in the combat zone and requested the ground control for a vector to another target. With its P-37 still in operation, the controller announced one, 36km (19.5nm) away. This time, the Iraqi pilot decided to ripple-fire one R-40RD and one R-40TD, and thus make sure he would score a hit even if his opponent might deploy strong electronic countermeasures.[33]

Several A-6Es of VA-35 were still around – now all disengaging in a southern direction – as was their MiG-sweep, including VF-74's F-14A+s crewed by LCDR John 'Sherm' Sherman and LT David 'Biz' Bisaillon, and (in 162925/AA100) LT Scott 'Shaggy' Alwine and LCDR Dan 'Tarps' Cloyd. The two Tomcats approached Assad AB from the south, then made a big circle towards the east, south, and then west. Unlike Jones and Slade, they were underway at an even higher altitude – 10,668m (35,000ft) – at much higher speed, and thus in a better position to evade any kind of threat. They saw several SA-2s going ballistic, then heard Panigall's report that his HVU-escort was down, before receiving a radio call from the XO of VA-35, reporting there was a MiG-25 slicing through his formation in the direction of Assad AB, before turning around to chase him. The Intruder dived for the deck, and the MiG gave up. Alwine described what happened next:

> Things seemed to quiet down and I was thinking of Boots and Rat, when we got a single audible radar warning alert. I looked at the scope and just stared at it: it showed a spike from our dead 6 o'clock, but not by any of the surface-to-air threats I had been seeing all week. Traps got me moving with a "Break right!" call...[34]

A view of the forward part of F-14A+ BuNo 162925, Modex AA100 – the Tomcat flown by Alwine and Cloyd during a dogfight with an Iraqi MiG-25 early on 21 January 1991. Notable in the foreground right is the usual mix of air-to-air missiles, including – from top towards the bottom – an AIM-9, an AIM-7M, and (lower right corner) one of the big AIM-54Cs.

As of 1991, this MiG-25PD – IrAF serial number 25211 – was operated by No. 96 Squadron. This photograph shows it after being captured by US troops in 2003, with a dismounted wing. (Tom Cooper Collection)

Alwine wrenched his Tomcat into a max-performance turn to the right, all the time keeping an eye on the RHAW-display: the spike followed them from six to four o'clock, despite Cloyd dispensing chaff all the time. The hard manoeuvre and chaff did their job when the threat was on their three o'clock. The loss of the target disturbed Ibrahim for several seconds, until he realised there was another target in front of him: contrary to Alwine and Cloyd, Sherman and Bisaillon opted to light their afterburners, unload and accelerate straight ahead, away from the threat. The Iraqi was busy locking on and seconds away from opening fire when Alwine and Cloyd returned to the scene:

We continued the right turn, and I started pulling the nose up, until I saw a MiG, high on our right side. Nose, wing, tail lights on! We pulled him into our HUD and I selected AIM-9 (no radar). Got a good self-track and tone. Best I could tell, we were at his 1 o'clock, a little below but climbing. Traps called AWACS with our position and contact info and asked for a declaration. As we continued, we were level, nose-on, 80 degrees angle of bank, about 2,000ft range, now at his 2 o'clock, but sweeping quickly towards his wing-line – when our RHAW lit up, completely saturated with energy from his side lobes and lock-on on Sherm! In a pre-dawn light at 30,000ft, I was able to see that his canopy was flush with his fuselage and the dim light to the east highlighted his oxygen hose, snaking from his mask down into the cockpit. Naively, for a second I thought it might be an F-111, which was ridiculous because no F-111s were anywhere around, and radar indications were for an air-to-air radar. Traps called for a belly check to honour the radar warning and make sure we were not turning in front of his wingman. Belly-checked clear but we lost a lot of geometry and were now at his 5 o'clock. Nevertheless, the AIM-9 held lock the whole time. We fell into trail, not sure of the exact range. The AIM-9 seeker kept oscillating between the left and the right engine, with as solid a tone as I've ever heard. Traps called AWACS again for declaration. I'll never forget the controllers reply: "Identify if able!" This might sound silly, but in less than 20 seconds, I went from very fearful to very comfortable. Belly checked clear, no radar warning indications, Sherm and Biz clear, and a solid weapons solution! We intended to literally pull up to the contact, pull out a flashlight and see who were we dealing with.'

Converted from hunter to prey in a matter of seconds, at this moment the Iraqi pulled his stick into a lap, taking his opponent by surprise, as described by Alwine:

I had AIM-9, active AIM-54, or guns as my best options. My thumb was already on the weapon selector when, all of a sudden, my entire HUD was full of a MiG! He pulled up and then left, very aggressively. We were VERY close. I instinctively selected gun as he rolled right and pulled hard again. We overshot in the vertical but then mimicked his manoeuvre: I was now pulling right to the edge of buffet in the thin air, desperately trying to reel him back into my HUD. We were overbanked, about 135 degrees, and pulling through west towards northwest. Then, as I started fishing for an AIM-9 tone, he disappeared: flew into the cloud layer. I unloaded to just under 1g to accelerate after him, but, as we broke through the clouds, we were completely inundated with cultural lightning: the tiny red tail light was lost in the sea of ground clutter.

Now well separated from their wingman, and dozens of miles behind the strike package, Alwine and Cloyd found themselves all alone and heading the 'wrong way'. There was no other option but turning south to meet one of the tankers over Saudi Arabia.

CLAIMS AND COUNTER-CLAIMS

Even if the above-described Iraqi accounts have never been published, they seem to perfectly match the widely published accounts by Jones and Slade, and depict the only loss of an F-14 Tomcat during the Second Gulf War. With hindsight, the story about the Tomcat being shot down by an SA-2 seems unsupportable: even if deploying its D20 missiles in 'optical mode', Saleh's SA-2 SAM site still had to paint their target with radar before doing so, while neither Panigall's EA-6B nor the RHAW gear of Jones' and Slade's F-14A+ recorded any kind of SAM-related emissions. Furthermore, there was no way for Saleh to 'optically' guide his missiles to a target flying above a solid overcast, and – contrary to what is said in some circles – his D20 missiles were also not equipped with any kind of a 'secondary IR-homing system'. Even then, the chances of his missiles actually scoring a hit on a target operating at the very edge of their range, were less than slim. Furthermore, not only when reporting the shoot-down of the escorting Tomcat on the radio, but

Modex 200 and a dark grey star on the fin identified this F-14A as the 'CAG-bird' (the jet officially assigned to the commander of CVW-1) of VF-33. Nicknamed the 'Starfighters', the squadron had its own share of 'fleeting encounters' with IrAF interceptors during the last week of January 1991.

A division of F-14s seen refuelling from a big KC-10A Extender tanker of the USAF. Notably, these four Tomcats belonged to no fewer than three different squadrons: in the foreground is AA207 from VF-33, flying wing to AJ202 from VF-84. In the background are two F-14As from VF-14. (Photo by CDR David Parsons)

also in their post-mission de-brief, Panigall's crew clearly recalled an Iraqi Foxbat appearing behind them, and were actually surprised that this did not attack them. Although their recollections have been supported by multiple Intruder crews from VA-35 until the present day, no USN officials were ready to believe them: Jones and Slade were declared to have been shot down by a SAM.

Ironically, the High Command of the IrAF eventually followed in fashion and officially credited Saleh and the 62nd Missile Battery with a Tomcat kill. On the contrary, while Lieutenant-Colonel Nabil was subsequently decorated and, after the war, assigned as the CO No. 6 Squadron, his claim was entirely ignored, just as Ibrahim was never decorated for his actions on 17, 18 or 21 January 1991.[35]

STARFIGHTER IN TROUBLE

During the night of 21 to 22 January, the CAOC changed its strategy by ordering a series of strikes on Iraqi air bases. Instead of runways, fighter-bombers began targeting the hardened aircraft shelters housing enemy jets with laser-guided bombs (LGBs). This was something the IrAF was unable to counter: despite the partial success of that day, it ceased resisting strikes on its facilities in the west. Instead, it ordered an evacuation of the remaining aircraft to air bases north of Baghdad from where the most advanced of them were to subsequently be flown out to the safety of Iran. With a single blow, the Navy's Tomcats thus found themselves entirely out of targets: henceforth, it was only occasionally that they would catch any enemy aircraft on their radars. One such case almost resulted in another loss of an F-14.

Late on 27 January, CO VF-33, CDR Dale 'Snort' Snodgrass, led a MiG-sweep in front of a CVW-1 airstrike against a powerplant north of Baghdad. Well inside Iraq, Snodgrass's AWG-9 picked up two contacts, and the aggressive pilot promptly pushed after them. Of course, warned by their SPS-15s, both Iraqi MiG-29 pilots turned around and 'ran' – straight for the nearest SAM concentration. Underway at an altitude of about 7,620m (25,000ft) above a solid undercast and almost supersonic, Snodgrass pressed on until finding himself under fire from multiple SAM sites. To his good fortune, he and his RIO took a look at the area of sky to see a missile approaching them: the pilot rolled his Tomcat into an 8-10g turn into the threat, deploying chaff as he went: the manoeuvre was successful in breaking the lock, and causing the missile to detonate behind him, but the F-14A loaded with six missiles and two drop tanks then lost the right engine. While trying to re-light, Snodgrass descended to less than 3,048m (10,000ft) and decelerated, thus finding himself under heavy anti-aircraft fire. Struggling to get the necessary airflow, he engaged minimal afterburner to re-light the right engine, was successful, and then climbed back to safety in full afterburner. This 'close call' was the last known case in which an F-14 operating from the three carriers deployed in the Red Sea is known to have had a contact with an airborne IrAF fighter over western Iraq during the Second Gulf War.[36]

6
ACTION FROM THE PERSIAN GULF

While the action of the three airwings embarked on aircraft carriers underway in the Red Sea resulted in most of the Navy's encounters with Iraqi interceptors and thus caught most attention, the aircraft carriers underway in the Persian Gulf were no less busy. Indeed, it was from this area of operations that the first of the USN's manned airstrikes on Iraq was launched, when 20 A-6Es from CVW-5 (USS *Midway*) hit Wahda AB in southern Iraq and al-Jabr AB in Kuwait early on 17 January 1991. Intruders from CVW-2 (USS *Ranger*) were soon to follow. However, unlike the 1st and 2nd ADSs of the Kari, because of their proximity to Kuwait the 3rd (South) and the 5th (Kuwait) ADSs were heavily hit by a mass of Coalition airstrikes right from the start of the war. Not only were the runways of the main IrAF air base in this area – Ali Ibn Abu Talib AB (colloquially known as 'Tallil' in the West) – severely cratered, but the four MiG-25s and seven MiG-29s forward-deployed at Jaliba Forward Operating Base (FOB), for example, never managed to fly even a single sortie. A handful of other interceptors scrambled had too little space to manoeuvre and their pilots were mostly forced to divert to air bases further north. As a consequence, the Iraqi resistance was quickly reduced to the local SAM and anti-aircraft artillery sites fighting their own battles for survival. Eventually, the Navy's Tomcats were left with very little to do.

ALMOST A FRATRICIDE

As over western Iraq, the intensity of engagements between Navy and Iraqi aircraft over southern Iraq was dependent on the methods of attack employed by A-6E Intruder crews. Unlike the USAF, where there was the practice of higher echelons dictating tactics to unit commanders, in the US Navy there was a strong aversion against such methods of command. Thus, individual units were left to decide how to attack. Initially, like VA-35 on board USS *Saratoga*, Intruder crews of VA-115 and VA-185 aboard USS *Midway* were firmly convinced that nocturnal attacks from low altitude were their best option. The crews of VA-145 and VA-155 of CVW-2 (not 'embarked') shared this opinion, and flew their early air strikes in the same fashion. The Iraqis did not attempt a single interception against their operations over Kuwait and the Basra area. However, with hindsight, it is possible that this was a good omen, because the communication and coordination between the Coalition forces over part of the battlefield was anything other than perfect. For example, during the first day of the war, Navy E-2Cs reported 'MiG-29s' in orbit near Ali Ibn Abu Talib AB – only to later find out these were USAF F-15s. In several other cases, F-14s had to de-conflict with each other with the help of their fighter-fighter data-links. Ultimately, because Tomcats were rarely sent into MiG-sweeps

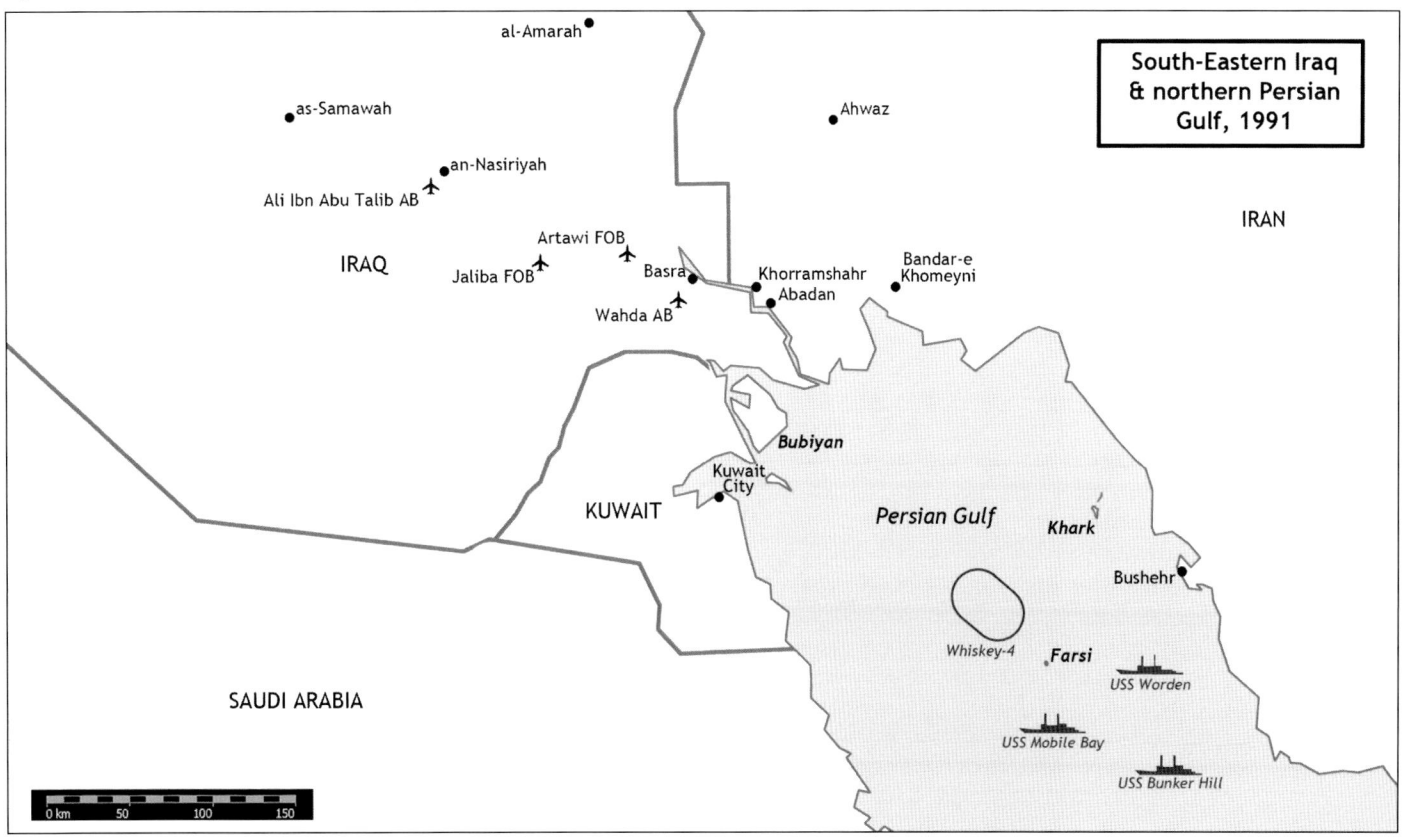

A map of the northern Persian Gulf and southern Iraq, with the most important CAP-station and the positions of the Navy's major anti-aircraft-warfare ships. (Map by Tom Cooper)

An F-14A of VF-2 streaking low over USS *Ranger* (CV-61) in the Persian Gulf during Operation Desert Shield in autumn 1990. During the Second Persian Gulf War, this squadron flew not only CAPs over the Persian Gulf, but also MiG-sweeps, escort for Boeing B-52 Stratofortress bombers over southern Iraq, and reconnaissance with TARPS pods.

deeper over southern Iraq, they encountered no IrAF interceptors. One of VF-1's pilots was Stuart 'Meat' Broce, who flew three sorties on 17 January 1991, and summarised these as follows:

> Some Tomcats went along on strikes in Kuwait. I've got to CAP over the Gulf, to "delouse" the strike packages returning south. Lots of radar contacts, but all were just returning strike aircraft, some with IFF forgotten in the excitement. Joining up on supersonic targets at night to visually identify them turned out to be impractical. We were actually laughing at the futility of the entire exercise.[1]

IRAQI STRIKE ON ABAQIQ

Since the earlier operations of the Navy's Tomcat units were marred by such communication difficulties, it is unsurprising to observe that not only did the same happen once again on 24 January 1991, but that the Americans then experienced an interesting series of problems with their other equipment. On this day, the IrAF launched its sole offensive operation of the conflict. Based on an idea from August 1990, this was a plan to deploy Mirage F.1EQ-5s to hit the Saudi oil refinery in Ras Tanura, and an oil pumping station in al-Abaqiq, both on the coast of the Persian Gulf. Preoccupied with what was going on during the first days of war, the Deputy Operations IrAF took nearly a week before ordering the Abu Ubayida AB-based No. 81 and No. 89 Squadrons to prepare for this strike, late on 22 January 1991. With all available pilots volunteering to take part, the staff of both units were quick in sorting out the details and each squadron prepared a total of eight Mirages, as follows:[2]

- Ras Tanura: No. 89 Squadron, 2 Mirage F.1EQ-4s armed with two SAMP 400kg bombs and two R.550 Magics each,

This image taken by the TARPS-pod of an F-14A from VF-84 shows two ships at the southern approach to the Iraqi naval base in Umm Qassr.

and equipped with Remora and Sycomor pods; supported by 4 Mirage F.1EQ-4s acting as tankers and 2 Mirage F.1EQ-4s providing top cover up to Bubiyan Island
- Al-Abaqiq: No. 81 Squadron, 4 Mirage F.1EQ-5s armed with four SAMP 400kg bombs and two R.550 Magics each, supported by 4 Mirage F.1EQ-5s acting as tankers.

Iraqi Mirage F.1EQ pilots were not only experts in air combat in the BVR-regime, but also in low-altitude strike operations. This photograph shows a pair of F.1EQ-5s: notable are their IFR-probes – used frequently for attacks into Iran at earlier times, and once again on 24 January 1991. (Dassault)

The strike was originally scheduled for 23 January but had to be postponed because Abu Ubayida AB was heavily hit that morning and two Mirages destroyed inside their hardened aircraft shelters. The ground crews rapidly prepared replacement aircraft, but then one of these was hit in a new airstrike. Finally, the Iraqis launched at 17.00hrs, but then flew into such bad weather while approaching Basra, that the mission leader ordered everybody to abort. Back at Abu Ubayida AB, a decision was taken to start a new attempt the next morning. During the following night, the base was once again hit by RAF Tornados using JP.233 submunition pods. Ground crews thus spent hours cleaning mines sown down the taxiways and one of two runways. The mission was finally launched only once the runways were clear at 11.50. This time, the weather was favourable and, underway at an altitude of just 50m (164ft), the Mirages prepared to undertake

An Iraqi Mirage F.1EQ-4, equipped with a pair of RP.35 drop tanks and a 'buddy' refuelling pack under the centreline, streaming its drogue. The Iraqi Mirage pilots were intensively trained in buddy-buddy refuelling operations since 1986 and proved capable of running these at altitudes of only 50m (165ft)! (Dassault)

A Sparrow-armed F-14A of VF-84 as seen in company of a KC-135 tanker shortly after the end of Operation Desert Storm. The squadron flew its share of CAPs over the Persian Gulf and became involved in attempts to intercept a pair of Iraqi Mirage F.1EQ-4s underway to strike the oil pumping station in Abaqiq, in Saudi Arabia, on 24 January 1991.

their first planned IFR-operation after passing low over Basra. At this point in time, their mission began falling apart: no fewer than three of the tankers supporting the Abaqiq strike suffered technical malfunctions and could not transfer any fuel. Therefore, the CO of No. 81 Squadron was forced to return his entire formation back to Abu Ubayida AB. Tankers of No. 89 Squadron had all worked as expected, and this formation continued the mission: indeed, shortly after reaching the northern Persian Gulf, it undertook its second in-flight refuelling: while all of the other Mirages then peeled off, the two piloted by Major Ali Hussein Fadhil Obeidi and Captain Mohammad Saleem continued southbound.

Further south, an E-3 Sentry AWACS detected the formation of No. 81 Squadron before it reached Basra, but then misinterpreted its turning back north for a decoy move. Around 12.20hrs, it then detected Obeidi and Saleem's Mirages as these reached the Persian Gulf. At this time, the two jets were detected by a pair of F/A-18s from USS *Midway* and the Hornets attempted to intercept but lost the contact less than four minutes later. Just around the same time, the Mirages were then detected by a pair of F-14As from VF-84 on the Whiskey-4 CAP-station from about 60km (32nm) away. Because the radar of the guided missile cruiser USS *Worden* proved unable to hold the contact, the Tomcat crews were ordered to investigate. However, when the F-14s started their approach, their AWG-9s both lost the contact. In turn, it was now the next guided missile cruiser of the USN – USS *Mobile Bay* – to make fleeting contact with the approaching Iraqis: although the Aegis-equipped cruiser maintained the contact, by now the F-14s were unable to re-acquire on time to attack.[3]

Meanwhile, the AWACS – which was not in control of the Tomcats, nor in radio contact with them, and, due to technical difficulties, not transmitting its radar picture to the USN's warships – vectored in four RSAF F-15Cs instead. Ordered to investigate first, the Saudi pilots executed a 'Polish Heart' manoeuvre, which brought their flight-leader, Captain Ayedh ash-Shamrani, directly behind the two Iraqi Mirages. After identifying his opponents positively, he received permission to open fire and, at 12.34hrs, shot down both targets using AIM-9P Sidewinders. Captain Salmeem was killed outright, while Major Obeidi was badly injured on ejection: he was picked out of the Persian Gulf by a Saudi rescue helicopter, but later died in a hospital.[4]

LAST, BUT NOT LEAST

On 6 February 1991, two VF-1 crews were briefed to fly a HVU-escort for an EA-6B planned to jam SAM sites in southern Kuwait in support of a photo-reconnaissance mission. Lieutenant Scott 'Ash' Malynn was to fly with LT Dan 'Zimby' Zimberoff as RIO, while LT Stuart 'Meat' Broce was to pilot the second F-14A, with the CO VF-1, Ron 'Bongo' McElraft as RIO. Armed with four AIM-7M Sparrows and four AIM-9M Sidewinders each, the two Tomcats launched at about noon and headed north when, about ten minutes into the flight, the E-2 controller from VAW-116 called them to switch to another radio frequency for 'alternate tasking'. McElraft continued:

After we dialled up the new frequency, the new controller told us to go "covered": to turn on the voice scrambler. Then he gave us a new mission: we were to refuel over the northern part of the Gulf and proceed to a CAP station at the coordinates he gave us. I knew something was up when I heard the coordinates: the longitude seemed right but the latitude didn't. In my mirrors I could see my RIO trying to unfold his chart to get to an area we haven't been to before. The station was well up into Iraq, way north of Kuwait.

On the way to the tanker, we found out that our radar was not working. Our wingman's radar worked though, so we decided to proceed. Judging by the orders, I wonder if that was our option. I know that everyone in the flight felt the same as I did. This wouldn't be an "ordinary" flight. Since the start of the war, all but a few of our flights had been conducted entirely over water, and those that weren't involved only a few brief, wide-eyed minutes over land. We knew we were breaking new ground for all of the fighters in the Gulf.

As we flew from the tanker toward land, the weather got progressively worse. There were a few broken layers down below about 15,000ft and they seemed to get thicker up north. Needless to say, as we crossed the beach and headed inland, we were fast and high and jinking. We skirted Kuwait City to the north to avoid the known SAM sights. I had the lead and all our heads were on swivels. Just south of Basra, some white puffs appeared on the other side of my wingman who was flying about half a mile away. Some of their larger AAA was reaching our altitude, but either their aim was way off, or jinking was working.

We finally reached our station and started flying a racetrack pattern in hopes that Zimby could get a good picture on his radar. Nothing appeared. Meanwhile, I was scanning the ground through the clouds in an attempt to mark our position, and detect any sign of a missile launch. There was a small settlement, a river, and a few lakes in the area. I was also looking for any artillery, heavy equipment, revetments or any other military activity.

After about ten minutes on station, our controller broke the silence with "Wolfpack, engage bandit vector 210, 36 angels low, nose on!". This meant, 'hey, turn to a heading 210, destroy enemy aircraft 36 miles in that direction, flying low and heading for you!' I immediately passed the lead to Ash and Zimby because they had a radar and we didn't. We lit the afterburners and turned.

As the two Tomcats accelerated, and because the AWACS had never informed them about the nature of their target, Broce began mentally preparing himself for the 'worst case scenario': a clash with Iraqi MiG-29s. The pair of F-14s dashed ever further north-west, roughly along the western bank of the Tigris River:

AWACS calls came fast: The controller called off the bearing and range. The miles ticked off very rapidly. At ten miles, neither of us had a radar contact. We were screaming downhill through the cloud layers approaching the speed of sound. I had levelled off at 3,000ft and Ash was way below me about two miles away when the controller said "Merge plot!" meaning that one of us was occupying the same little blip on his radar screen. I was looking all over the place, jinking and flipping the jet from side to side, when skipper said "Come left!...Helicopter!". I threw the plane into a 7g turn for about 270 degrees and visually picked up a camouflaged helicopter flying past the little settlement at about 50ft and going pretty fast. It as a Soviet-built "Hip" armed transport. We don't use those and Iraq does, so I selected a Sidewinder, and pitched up and to his left. I rolled inverted and pulled the nose down towards the helicopter: I was still at warp speed and heading downhill fast, so I knew I had about two seconds to get a good missile tone and shoot. I did.

An F-14A of the VF-1, firing an AIM-9 low above the sea surface in a pre-1991-exercise – in a scene closely reminiscent of Broce and McElraft's encounter with an Iraqi Mi-8 on 6 February 1991. Of course, the Mi-17 kill was scored deep over south-eastern Iraq.

The Mi-17 killing F-14A BuNo 162603, Modx NE103, seen after return to the USA, with a kill marking under the cockpit and the nick-name 'EL COYOTE' applied low on the fin. (Milpix/Martin Hornliman Collection)

By this time, McElraft – a Vietnam War veteran – was primarily concerned by the low altitude to which Broce had descended in order to get a clear shot at the helicopter: 'I started worrying about pulling out. I said, "Meat, pull out." Next thing I heard, "woosh". NOW, pull! Boom!'5

Broce continued:

The missile took off with a big "whoosh". I pulled up hard to avoid hitting the ground, and watched the missile accelerate. Just as I started planning my next shot, the missile slammed into the helicopter. The helo violently erupted into a huge fireball and poured into the ground. The explosion engulfed the entire helicopter, including the main rotor. In apparent slow motion, a single main rotor blade flipped up and out in front of the huge cloud of fire and black smoke.

I lit the burners and went straight up. I didn't shut the afterburners off until I was above the clouds again. Ash and Zimby had turned toward our position and overflew the wreckage. They later said that there wasn't much left. We joined up overhead and headed back to the Gulf for more fuel. On the tanker, another jet from our squadron joined up. The pilot, Opus, apparently saw the empty missile rail on the left side of the jet because his eyes got big when he looked at it. Other than a failed attempt by our sister squadron to sink a boat with a Sidewinder, my shot had been the only air-to-air missile fired by any Navy aircraft based in the Persian Gulf so far.

As far as is known, the Mi-17 in question was piloted by Lieutenant-Colonel Ghanem Abdul Jabara ash-Shammari (from the Iraqi Army Aviation Corps), who was killed together with his crew of two. The two VF-1 jets spent the next three hours CAPping over Iraq, waiting for another vector that never came. Eventually, short on fuel, they withdrew toward south, joining two other Tomcats from the same squadron to refuel from a KC-135. Broce, McElraft, Malynn and Zimberoff returned to USS *Ranger* only after sunset: nevertheless, a swarm of people including the commanding officer of CVW-2 was waiting to congratulate them: finally, the Navy had got the first confirmed aerial victory for its Tomcats in this war.

7
FINAL ENGAGEMENTS

For more than a decade after the end of the Second Persian Gulf War, F-14 Tomcats of the US Navy continued prowling the skies over northern and southern Iraq. During this time, the fleet experienced several fundamental changes. Ironically, the same was true for what was left of the Iraqi Air Force after the catastrophe that befell it in 1991. Following years of 'shadow boxing', the two opponents clashed in a series of fleeting engagements for the last time in 1999.

BIG ENGINES AND DIGITAL TOMCAT

Between 1987 and 1991, 38 newly-manufactured F-14A+s were delivered to the USN and 47 old F-14As were upgraded to the same standard – including F110-GE-400 engines and the ALR-67 RHAW-system – and, as described above, many of these saw operational service during Desert Shield and Desert Storm. Under the plan from 1985, in 1990 Grumman was then to switch to the production of the ultimate variant; the F-14D. Like the F-14A+/B, this was powered by F110-GE-400 engines but also included a completely reworked avionics suite. The AWG-9 received digital processing components from the F-15E's AN/APG-70, to become the AN/APG-71, which came with new working modes, significantly improved detection capabilities, tracking ranges, resolution, and the NCTR. The chin-installation that used to contain only the AAX-1 TCS was expanded through the addition of the AAS-42 IRST, while both cockpits received new digital displays (including a big HUD in the front). However, the end of the Cold War in 1989 resulted in massive budget cuts. Correspondingly, instead of 400 new Tomcats, the Navy received only 59 F-14Ds, of which four were test aircraft, 37 newly-manufactured, and 18 old F-14As upgraded to the new standard. The last Tomcat was delivered to the Navy on 10 July 1992.[1]

Another major change caused by the massive budget cuts of the 1990s was that the Navy was forced to disband no fewer than ten Tomcat squadrons: as a result, by 1995, most airwings retained only one unit of – frequently – only ten operational aircraft. Perhaps more importantly, as a consequence of experiences from the Second Persian Gulf War of 1991 – when, after quickly winning aerial supremacy and then full aerial superiority over Iraq, Navy Tomcat squadrons were left with very little to do – during the mid-1990s the Tomcat-community took care to adapt its mounts to the strike

The wreckage of one of seven MiG-29s forward-deployed at Jaliba FOB, as seen after the end of the Second Persian Gulf War. Together with at least one MiG-21, one Su-25, and two other MiG-29s, the jet was found by elements of the 24th (Mechanized) Infantry Division of the US Army while still fully intact in late March 1991, though surrounded by dozens of mines released by JP.233 dispensers carried by RAF Tornado GR.Mk 1s. After reporting the finding of 'few small sports aircraft', the troops destroyed them all by throwing hand-grenades into their cockpits. A few days later, the specialists of the Foreign Technologies Division of the USAF then visited the place to extract whatever 'interesting' pieces of wreckage were still around. (US DoD)

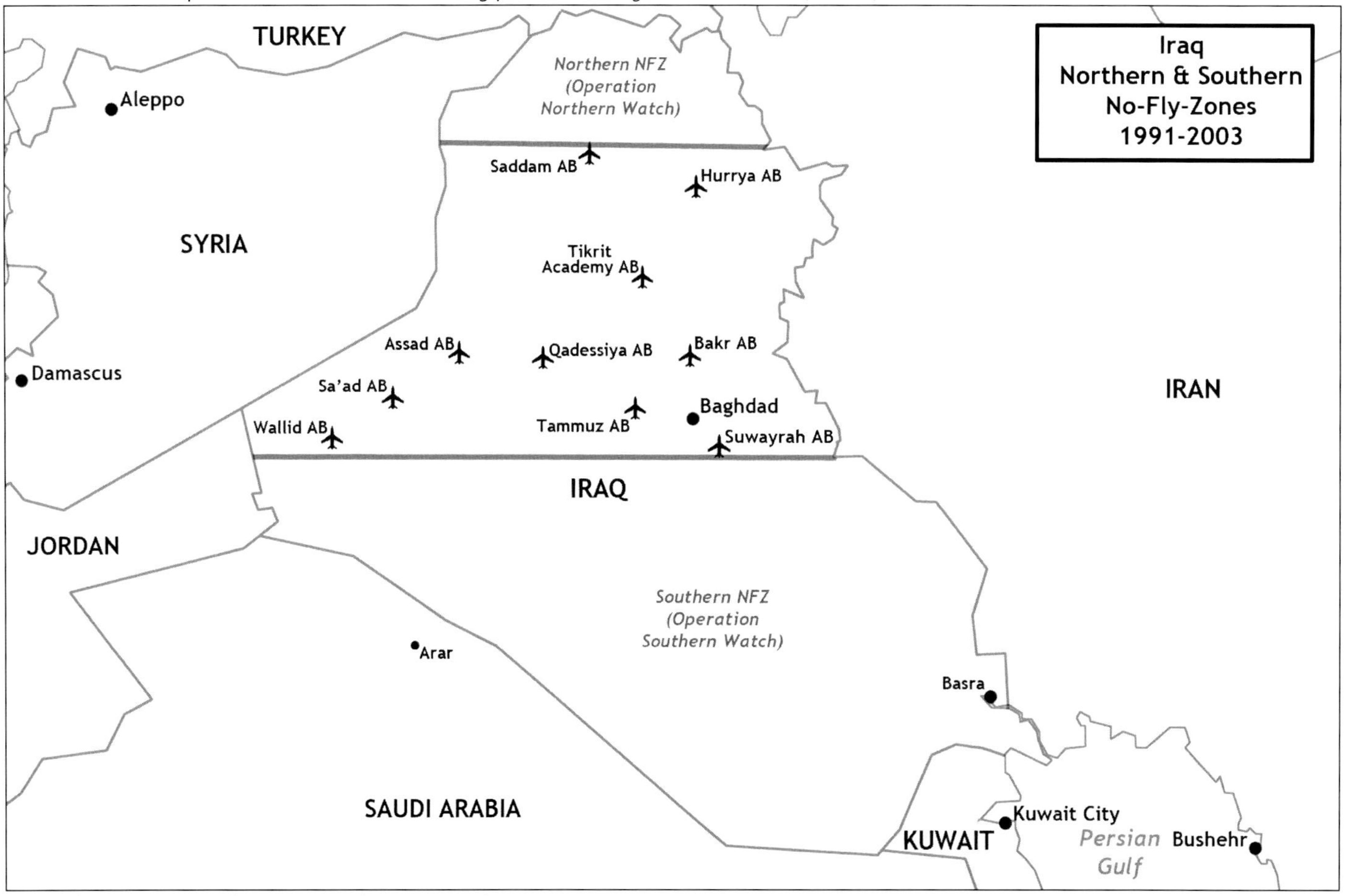

A map of NFZs over Iraq in the 1990s. (Map by Tom Cooper)

Tomcats of the USN continued patrolling the Iraqi skies for more than a decade after the end of Operation Desert Storm. This photograph shows an F-14A from VF-114 underway low over one of the ruined air bases in Kuwait in April 1991.

A trio of F-14As from VF-41 (centre and background), and VF-84, seen while refuelling from a KC-135 high above northern Iraq in April 1991.

role, i.e. the deployment of free-fall and then laser-guided bombs. Correspondingly, during Operation Deliberate Force over Bosnia, in late August and September 1995, the F-14As of the VF-41 flew their first ground attacks. The most dramatic related improvement was meanwhile in the making in the form of the adaptation of a slightly modified variant of the AN/AAQ-14 LANTRIN targeting pod to the Tomcat: first applied in 1995 by VF-103 (which subsequently took over the traditions of the disbanded VF-84 Jolly Rogers) and then the rest of the fleet, this resulted in the Tomcat becoming one of the most potent strike platforms in the US armed forces.

IRAQI NO-FLY ZONES

After the end of Operation Desert Storm, two major uprisings erupted in Iraq. Both were suppressed in brutal campaigns by the Iraqi armed forces. Because this was an 'internal affair' of the country, the USA and allies could do very little to help until the Iraqis reactivated their air force and began flying airstrikes against the insurgents. In response, the United Nations (UN) authorised the establishment of two no-fly zones (NFZs):

- The northern extended from the 36th parallel to the Turkish border,

- The southern was south of the 32nd parallel, but, in 1996, expanded to the 33rd parallel.

Reminiscent of the 'air policing' of the RAF and the Iraqi Air Force of the 1920s and the 1930s, both NFZs were maintained exclusively with air power: the northern by aircraft operating from NATO's air bases in Turkey, and the southern by aircraft operating from air bases in Kuwait, Saudi Arabia, and aircraft carriers underway in the Persian Gulf. Initially, the Iraqis did not challenge the NFZ, but this began to change in 1992, when IrAF did try to disrupt some related operations – only to lose one of its MiG-25s to the then brand-new AIM-120A fired by a General Dynamics (later Lokcheed-Martin) F-16 of the USAF.

COLLECTING PIECES

Having its air bases and the combat fleet shredded to pieces, and the mass of its best aircraft evacuated to Iran and then impounded during the Second Persian Gulf War, the IrAF was forced into a major reorganisation. The number of operational squadrons was decreased from 43 to 33 by 1992. When the remaining MiG-21s and MiG-29s were withdrawn from service in 1995 (because both fleets were experiencing issues with their engines, airframes were out of resources, and the Iraqis possessed no capacity to overhaul them at home) additional units were disbanded. Essentially, the entire IrAF interceptor fleet was now down to two squadrons of MiG-23s, one squadron of MiG-25s, and two of Mirage F.1s. Even then, many of the about 50 remaining airframes were in need of overhauls and upgrades to remain operational, or retain any kind of operational value. Doing what they could with the tools and equipment to hand, the Iraqis launched an all-out attempt to resurrect their fighter fleet – with mixed results.

While the number of fully mission capable MiG-23MLs, MiG-25PD/PDSs and Mirage F.1EQs was kept stable for several years, more ambitious projects had to be abandoned. One of these was related to the Iraqi realisation that the E-2 Hawkeye AEW and E-3 Sentry AWACS aircraft of the US Navy and the US Air Force respectively, played the primary role in the US and allied ability to maintain the NFZs. It drove the Iraqis to attempt to modify one of their MiG-25RBs (a strike-reconnaissance variant) through the installation of the Soviet/Russian Fantasmagoria anti-radar targeting system and related Kh-58 (ASCC/NATO-code AS-11 Kilter) anti-

A trio of IrAF Mirages that survived the carnage of 1991, seen next to a hardened aircraft shelter at Shayka Mazhar FOB in late March 1991 – in a photograph taken by the TARPS-pod of an F-14A from VF-2.

radar missiles. Although one Foxbat was stripped down pending such a modification, the work was never completed because of the next major showdown with the USA starting in 1998.[2]

OPERATION DESERT FOX

The primary point of disagreement between Iraq and the USA, and its allies, during the 1990s was the UN Security Council's resolutions under which Baghdad was obliged to permit inspections of its nuclear, biological, and chemical (NBC) warfare facilities by the United Nations Special Commission (UNSCOM) inspectors. Initially, Iraq accepted UNSCOM inspections, and these dismantled all of its NBC installations and weaponry. However, when the USA and allies insisted on additional inspections, Baghdad refused to permit these. Therefore, on 16 December 1998, the USA and Great Britain launched Operation Desert Fox, aiming to further 'degrade' Iraq's ability to manufacture weapons of mass destruction. In addition to USAF aircraft operating from bases in Saudi Arabia, Bahrain, United Arab Emirates, and Oman, Operation Desert Fox involved the aircraft of CVW-3, now deployed aboard the nuclear-powered aircraft carrier USS *Enterprise* (CVN-65). Another nuclear-powered aircraft carrier, USS *Carl Vinson* (CVN-71), with aircraft of CVW-11 embarked, arrived a day after the fighting began. Eventually, 650 sorties against 275 targets were flown, of which 211 were hit by guided bombs: the Pentagon reported the destruction of 9 command facilities and damage to a further 11, 32 SAM sites, 13 industrial facilities and 18 factories.[3]

In the aftermath of Operation Desert Fox, Baghdad announced that it would no longer respect the NFZs and resumed its efforts to shoot down a Coalition aircraft. Correspondingly, the IrAF began deploying its SAM sites and then IrAF interceptors within both zones. This resulted in a series of short but sharp skirmishes. For example, on 28 December 1998, the Iraqis deployed three SAM sites near Mosul and opened fire at a formation of USAF F-15Es: the Americans hit back with LGBs and reported the destruction of all of the Iraqi launchers. Three days later, the IrAF deployed a single SA-6 SAM site all the way to Ali Ibn Abu Talib AB, south of Nassiriyah, and nearly shot down a Tornado GR.Mk 1 of the RAF. This time the USAF reacted by deploying a sizeable formation of F-16s – escorted by Navy EA-6Bs – to destroy the site with LGBs. Enraged, on 3 January 1999 Saddam increased the pressure by ordering several MiG-23s, MiG-25s, and Mirages into the southern NFZ. Because the jets in question operated only whenever there were no E-2Cs or E-3Cs around, the Americans and allies failed to intercept them. It thus took the setting of a carefully prepared 'trap' for the Iraqis to enter the engagement envelope of US interceptors.

USS *Carl Vinson* with aircraft of CVW-11 on deck. Together with those from the famous USS *Enterprise*, the crews from this aircraft carrier played a crucial role in Operation Desert Fox. Only a few weeks later, two F-14 Tomcat crews from CVW-11's VF-213 became the first USN crews to ever deploy the AIM-54C Phoenix missile in anger.

A series of pre- and post-strike reconnaissance photographs of one of targets struck during Operation Desert Fox, as released by the US Department of Defence.

PHOENIX SHOTS

Early on the morning of 5 January 1999, two AIM-54C-armed F-14Ds of VF-213 were sent over southern Iraq, together with a division of AIM-120 armed F/A-18Cs. The Tomcats were crewed by LCDR Vince 'Bluto' Sparito and LCDR Bob 'Jumby' Castleton (in BuNo 163903, Modex NH107) and LT Jonathan 'Shoe' Shoemaker and LT Mike 'BuFi' Bilzor (BuNo 159619, Modex NH106). The Iraqi interceptors had been active over the southern NFZ since dawn, and one of their formations had been engaged by a flight of F-15Cs of the USAF: the latter fired one AIM-7M Sparrow and three AIM-120 Slammers from long range, but all missiles missed. About 15 minutes later, another Iraqi formation appeared: two MiG-23MLs led by Lieutenant-Colonel Hassan al-Hashemawi from No. 93 Squadron scrambled from Suwaira airfield, both equipped with Remora ECM-pods. As soon as the Tomcats turned into them, the ground control advised both Iraqis to turn around and head back to their base, attempting to entice their enemy to follow into an ambush. The AWACS detected all three Iraqi jets and cleared the Tomcat and Hornet pilots to fire. When the F-14s engaged, the Iraqis scrambled a MiG-25 that accelerated to Mach 1.5. The Tomcats, meanwhile underway at Mach 1.2, an altitude of 12,192m (40,000ft), and about 130km (70nm) in front and north-west of the Hornets, turned into the new threat and engaged: the lead F-14D fired one AIM-54C, followed by the wingman, who fired the second. However, because of being incorrectly armed

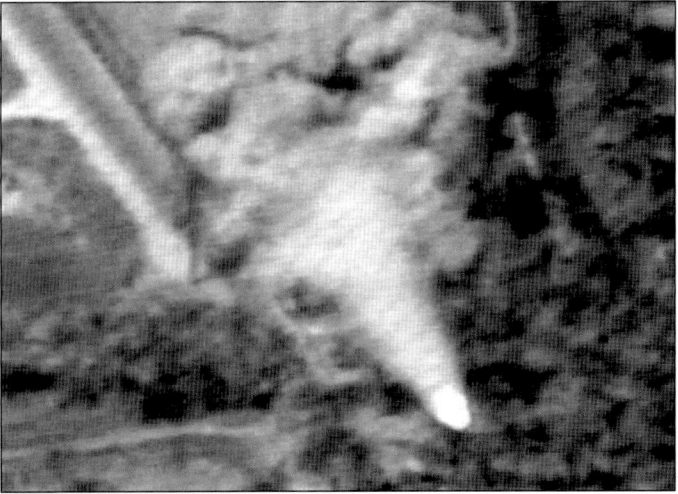

A still from a video released by the US Department of Defence, showing an Iraqi SA-3 SAM site firing at US aircraft underway over the southern NFZ.

before the two jets were launched from the deck of the USS *Carl Vinson*, both Phoenix missiles plunged to the ground, without ever activating their engines. The Foxbat kept coming for a while longer, but the Tomcat crews were advised not to go for a merge: instead, they disengaged towards the south.[4]

In the meantime, two F/A-18s from VFA-22 and VFA-97 were vectored north in an attempt to cut off the two MiG-23MLs that

The F-14D NH107 seen on the deck of USS Carl Vinson, after return from the engagement on 5 January 1999. Note the AIM-54C missing from the left underwing station.

were dashing away at supersonic speed in the direction of Baghdad. Although approaching to about 130km from their opponents, the Navy pilots concluded they could not run them down: both thus disengaged towards the south. By this time, both MiG-23MLs were critically short on fuel and Hashemawi thus led them into an emergency landing at Rashid AB, which had not been an active air base since the mid-1980s. The leader landed safely, but his wingman, Major Fallah Mahdi al-Azzawi overshot on his first attempt and was forced to fly a circle: while approaching for his second landing attempt, his aircraft ran out of fuel, stalled and crashed only 200 metres short of the runway, killing the unlucky pilot. Although never claimed as an official kill by the USN, the commander of the CVW-11, CAPT James T Knight, drew a logical conclusion: 'Screw him – a kill is a kill.'

Later the same year, and following another series of similar skirmishes, it was CVW-2 that attempted to set up another ambush. Operating from USS Constellation (CV-64), on 14 September 1999 VF-2 launched a single F-14D – BuNo 164349, Modex NE102 – crewed by LCDR Coby 'Coach' Loessberg with LCDR Michael 'Spock' McMillan. Acting as a wingman was a single F/A-18C from VFA-151, piloted by LT Ron 'Semi' Candiloro.[5] The two jets had spent three hours on the CAP station when two MiG-23MLs appeared out of Tammuz AB. Loessberg turned into the threat, accelerating as he went – while trying not to leave the slower Hornet too far behind. Then, using the (much-improved) Link-16 datalink, he and his RIO obtained their targeting data from the supporting E-2C, powered up their APG-71 and quickly set up an AIM-54C launch. Because his jet was not yet equipped with Link-16, Candiloro was taken by surprise when he saw the big Phoenix missile separating from the Tomcat and stampeding up and away. Finally recognising the threat, both MiGs promptly broke and turned away towards the north, doing their best to exit the engagement envelope of the AIM-54. Loessberg concluded:

The F-14D BuNo 164349, Modex NE102 was the Tomcat flown by Loessberg and McMillan during their engagement with a pair of Remora-equipped MiG-23MLs on 14 September 1999.

An F-14D of VF-2 as seen seconds after a catapult launch, low next to the bow of USS *Constellation*.

A 'buffalo on the run': an AIM-54 accelerating away from the releasing F-14 during a training shot.

The Phoenix missed because they turned and ran not long after we fired. This was confirmed via IRST. The shot was not taken in the heart of the envelope. Had we been able to achieve the optimum speed and altitude at launch we might have been able to improve our probability-of-kill.

The MiGs headed north, we were approaching the border of the NFZ, and I knew my wingman was rapidly approaching bingo fuel state. We were a defensive counter-air mission so we accomplished our mission.

Once we were safely heading south and knew there was no longer a threat, I had to quickly get on the optimum flight profile to safely get Semi back to the S-3 tankers that were waiting for us. I do remember being a little concerned about that and communicating to the E-2 the urgency of having a tanker waiting for him.[6]

CONCLUSIONS

Designed by Grumman to outmanoeuvre small and nimble MiGs, deployed by the US Navy to fight 'hordes' of Soviet cruise missile-armed bombers in all-out battles of a war that never took place, the F-14 Tomcat eventually saw plenty of action – but, in a kind of conflict it was hardly expected to fight: in so-called 'local' wars. While clashes with interceptors and fighter-bombers of the Libyan Arab Air Force of 1981 and 1989 made it a sort of star, the Tomcat's action against Iran in 1987, and it ultimate performance during the biggest war in which it served – the one against Iraq of 1991 – has largely evaded public attention. The discussion about why it did not score as many (hard) kills as USAF's F-15s did in 1991, is likely to go on for years, perhaps even decades to come: however, after a closer look, there is no denial that USN's F-14s did score – and heavily at that. The issue is that the results of all the efforts by their crews are less obvious. These become clear only when one considers the 'shadow boxing' over western Iraq during the daylight hours of 17 January 1991. The IrAF had at least ten interceptors either airborne or in the process of scrambling when the first of the Navy's formations approached Wallid AB, but, with the exception of two – which then flew into Hornets – none managed to engage. Indeed, most of the Iraqi pilots decided to disengage. Similarly, the IrAF had up to 12 or 16 interceptors airborne over Sa'ad AB alone, yet not one of these engaged the incoming Navy formation. In both cases, all turned away *before* facing the four F-14s of the MiG-sweep element. While thus left without (hard) kills, the involved Tomcats scored a massive number of 'soft' kills – without firing a single shot. At least as significant was that thanks to these early victories, the situation largely remained that way for the rest of the Second Persian Gulf War, and for years afterwards.

This is even more important considering the level of proficiency and combat experience of the Iraqi pilots: like the crew of the sole Iranian F-4E encountered by the VF-21 section in August 1987, they were some of the most dangerous opponents that USN crews could face at the time, better versed in deploying their equipment to advantage than many other protentional opponents of this period. Although perfectly aware of the vast superiority of the F-14 in regards of technology and firepower, they were willing to fight: in most of cases, it was their ground controllers that ordered them to disengage.

Eventually, this – as well as one almost certain kill scored against an Iraqi MiG-25 on the evening of 17 January 1991, and a probable loss of an F-14A+ to a MiG-29 on the morning of 21 January 1991 – might change little in the way the Tomcat might go down in history. However, even in the 'grand picture', there is no denial that the efforts and experiences of all the crews involved – those flying F-14s, and those finding themselves in Tomcat's 'claws' – were, are, and are going to remain too precious to be ignored.

BIBLIOGRAPHY

Armistead, E. L., *AWACS and Hawkeyes: The Complete History of Airborne Early Warning Aircraft* (St Paul: MBI Publishing, 2002).

Baker, R., *Grumman F-14 Tomcat* (Ramsbury: The Crowood Press Ltd., 1998).

Becker, H.-J., 'Der Große Bluff: Die Geschichte der Tupolev Tu-98 Backfin', *Jet & Prop Extra*, 03/2002.

Brown, C., *Debrief: A Complete History of U. S. Aerial Engagements 1981 to the Present* (Atglen: Schifffer Publishing Ltd., 2007).

Brown, D. F., *Tomcat Alley: A Photographic Roll Call of the Grumman F-14 Tomcat* (Atglen: Schiffer Military Publishing, 1998; ISBN: 0-7643-0477-1)

Bugos, G. E., *Engineering the F-4 Phantom II: Parts into Systems* (Shrewsbury: Airlife Publishing, 1996).

Buttler, T., 'Steps to the Big League: US VFX and FX Programmes', *Air Enthusiast* No. 120, November/December 2005.

Calka, J.-P., Moreau, É., *F-100DÜ/F Super Sabre en Service dans l'Armée de l'Air* (EM37Éditions, 2010; ISBN: 978295375140)

Cooper, T. & Sipos, M., *Iraqi Mirages: The Dassault Mirage Family in Service with the Iraqi Air Force, 1981-1988* (Warwick: Helion & Co., 2019).

Cooper, T., *MiG-23 Flogger in the Middle East: Mikoyan I Gurevich MiG-23 in Service in Algeria, Egypt, Iraq, Libya and Syria, 1973-2018* (Warwick: Helion & Co., 2018).

Cooper, T., Sadik, Général de Brigade A., Bishop, F., *La guerre Iran-Irak: Les combat aériens, Hors-Serie Avions* No. 22 & No. 23 (Outreau: Éditions LELA PRESSE, 2007).

Dildy, Douglas C., Cooper, T., *F-15C Eagle vs MiG-23/25, Iraq 1991* (Oxford: Osprey Publishing, 2016).

Elward, B., 'RIO: The Role of Tomcat's Backseater', *Combat Aircraft*, July 1997.

Fomin, A., 'MiG-29 Evolution', *AirForces Monthly Profile No. 2: MiG-29 Fulcrum*, 2006.

Francillon, R. J., *Grumman Aircraft since 1929* (New York: Brassey's Inc., 1989).

Ghafouri, A., *Eagles of the Land of Iran, Volume 3* (in Farsi) (Tehran: Air Force Strategic Publishing, 2018)

Gilchrist, R., 'A Kill's a Kill', *fighterpilotpodcast.com*, April 2020

Gillcrist, Rear Admiral (USN, ret.,) P., *Tomcat! The Grumman F-14 Story* (Atglen: Schiffer Publishing Ltd., 1994).

Gunston, B., *American Warplanes* (London: Salamander Books Ltd., 1986).

Gunston, B., *An Illustrated Guide to Modern Fighters and Attack Aircraft* (London: Salamander Books Ltd., 1980).

Gunston, B., *An Illustrated Guide to Modern Soviet Air Force* (London: Salamander Books Ltd., 1982).

Gunston, B., *Modern Fighting Aircraft: F-111* (London: Salamander Books Ltd., 1983).

Holmes, T., *Grumman F-14 Tomcat: All Models, 1970-2006* (Yeovil: Haynes Publishing, 2018).

Hooton, E. R., Cooper, T. & Nadimi, F., *The Iran-Iraq War, Volume 1: The Battle for Khuzestan, September 1980-May 1982* (Revised Edition) (Warwick: Helion & Co., 2019).

Hooton, E. R., Cooper, T. & Nadimi, F., *The Iran-Iraq War, Volume 2: Iran Strikes Back, June 1982 – December 1986* (Revised Edition) (Warwick: Helion & Co. 2019).

Hooton, E., R., Cooper, T. & Nadimi, F., *The Iran-Iraq War, Volume 3: Iraq's Triumph* (Solihull: Helion & Co., 2017).

Hooton, E., R., Cooper, T. & Nadimi, F., *The Iran-Iraq War, Volume 4: The Forgotten Fronts* (Solihull: Helion & Co., 2018).

Jenkins, D. R., *Grumman F-14 Tomcat: Leading US Navy Fleet Fighter* (Leicester: Midland Publishing Ltd., 1997).

Lake, J., 'Mikoyan MiG-23/27 Flogger', *World Air Power Journal*, Vol. 8/Spring 1992.

Langston, B., 'Operation Praying Mantis: An Enterprise Combat Mission', *Naval Historical Foundation*, 14 April 2017

Liébert, M., Moreau, E., Defever, C., *Super Mystère B.2 en service dans l'armée de l'Air* (EM37 Editions, 2016; ISBN: 978-2-9537514-13)

Markovskiy, V., Perov, K., *Soviet Air-to-Air Rockets* (Moscow: Exprint Publishing Centre, 2005). (in Russian)

Menajul, Air Vice-Marshal S. W. B., Gunston, B., *Soviet War Planes* (London: Salamander Books Ltd., 1976).

Michel, M. L., *Clashes: Air Combat over North Vietnam, 1965-1972* (Annapolis: Naval Institute Press: 1997). Military-Industrial Group MAPO, *MiG-29 has no Equal in Air Combat* (Moscow: MAPO; 2006).

Mladenov, A., 'MiG-23MLD vs Western Fighters: The Soviet Air Force View', *Air Forces Monthly*, October 2003.

Mladenov, A., 'MiG-25 Foxbat', *Air International*, October 2006.

Morgan, R., *A-6 Intruder Units, 1974-96* (Combat Aircraft Series) (Oxford: Osprey, 2017).

Morgan, R., *Tip of the Spear: US Navy Carrier Units and Operations, 1974-2000* (Atglen: Schiffer Publishing, 2007).

Morse, S. (ed.), *Gulf Air War: Debrief* (London: Aerospace Publishing Ltd., 1991).

Pawloski, D., *Fighter Weapons Symposium, Book 1: Fighter Basics* (Fort Worth: Lockheed, internal publications for Lockheed Fort Worth Company and Customer Air Forces, 1995).

Pawloski, D., *Fighter Weapons Symposium, Book II: Changes in Threat Air Combat Doctrine and Force Structure* (Fort Worth: Lockheed, internal publications for Lockheed Fort Worth Company and Customer Air Forces, 1995).

Pawloski, D., *Fighter Weapons Symposium, Book III: Surface-to-Air Threats* (Fort Worth: Lockheed, internal publications for Lockheed Fort Worth Company and Customer Air Forces, 1995).

Peacock, L., *F-14 Tomcat* (Combat Aircraft Series No.5) (Oxford: Osprey, 1986).

Pokrant, M., *Desert Storm at Sea: What the Navy Really Did* (Santa Barbra: Greenwood Press, 1999)

Raspletin, Dr. A. A., *History PVO* (website in Russian: historykpvo.narod2.ru), 2013.

Richardson, D., Spick, M., *Modern Fighting Aircraft: F-4* (London: Salamander Books Ltd., 1984).

Sadik, Brigadier-General A., & Cooper, T., 'The First Night: Iraqi Air Force in Combat, 17 January 1991', *International Air Power Review*, Vol. 26/2009.

Spick, M. (ed.), *The Great Book of Modern Warplanes* (London: Salamander Books Ltd., 2000).

Spick, M., 'The Iron Tigers', *Air International*, June 1991.

Spick, M., *Modern Fighting Aircraft: F-14 Tomcat* (London: Salamander Books Ltd., 1985).

Sweetman, B., *Modern Fighting Aircraft: MiGs* (London: Salamander Books Ltd., 1985).

Sweetman, B., *Soviet Military Aircraft* (London: Hamlyn Publishing Ltd., 1981).

Taylor, M., *Naval Air Power* (Twickenham: Hamlyn Publishing, 1986).

Tokarev, M. Y., 'Kamikazes: The Soviet Legacy', *Naval War College Review*, Volume 67/No. 1, 2014

Wilcox, R. K., *Wings of Fury: From Vietnam to the Gulf War, the Astonishing True Stories of America's Elite Fighter Pilots* (New York: Pocket Books, 1996).

Woods, K., Pease, M. R., Stout, M. E., Murray, W., Lacey, J. G., *The Iraqi Perspective Report* (United States Joint Forces Command, 2006)

Woods, K., *The Mother of all Battles: Saddam Hussein's strategic plan for the Persian Gulf War* (Annapolis: Naval Institute Press, 2008).

DOCUMENTS

Iraqi Air Force & Air Defence Command, *List of Enemy Aircraft shot down in the Mother of All Battles* (self-published for internal use, 10 October 1991, translated from Arabic to English and provided by Brigadier-General Ahmad Sadik).

Iraqi Air Force & Air Defence Command, *Methods and Tactics employed by Enemy Air Forces during the Mother of All Battles* (self-published for internal use, 4 October 1991; excerpts translated from Arabic to English provided by Brigadier General Ahmad Sadik).

Iraqi Air Force & Air Defence Command, *The Role of the Air Force and Air Defence in the Mother of All Battles: After Action Report* (self-published for internal use, 5 November 1991, captured in 2003 and translated as 'A 1991 Dossier on the Role of the Iraqi Air Force in the Gulf War', by the US Department of Defence-sponsored Conflict Records Research Center (CRRC Record Number SH-AADF-D-000-396) in the course of the 'Project Harmony'.

Iraqi Ministry of Defence, *History of the Iraqi Armed Forces, Part 17; The Establishment of the Iraqi Air Force and its Development* (in Arabic), (Baghdad, Iraqi Ministry of Defence, 1988).

Office of Naval Intelligence, *NAVOPINTCEN SUITLAND MD message 250021Z: Request for Persian Gulf Related Info*, July 1987 (released under FOIA procedure).

Office of Naval Intelligence, *Speartip 009-88: Persian Gulf Fighter Developments*, 18 April 1988 (released under FOIA procedure).

Office of Naval Intelligence, *Speartip 014-90: Threat Posed to US/Allied Aircraft by Iraqi Fighter/Interceptors*, 1990 (exact date blotted out), (released under FOIA procedure).

NOTES

CHAPTER 1

1. Unless stated otherwise, this sub-chapter is based on Tokarev, *Kamikazes*.
2. Unless stated otherwise, this sub-chapter is based on Baker (1998); Bugos (1996); Buttler (2005); Gillcrist (1994); Gunston (*F-111*, 1983), Jenkins (1997); Peacock (1986); Richardson & Spick (1984); Spick (*F-14*, 1985); Spick, 'The Iron Tigers' (1991).
3. Before 1962, each of the US armed services has had its own designation system. The US Navy used to designate its aircraft by their purpose and their manufacturers. For example, F2F referred to the Grumman's (F) second (2) fighter (F) design; F3H to the McDonnell's (H) third (3) fighter (F) design. On 18 September 1962, a tri-service joint designation system was introduced for the Army, Navy, and Air Force, under which all the equipment was re-designated along its purpose only. For aircraft, the Pentagon adopted the USAF system, under which the first element was designating the purpose, the second the numerical type sequence, and sequential letter suffixes designated major modifications. For example, McDonnell-Douglas F4H-1 became the F-4B; Vought F8U the F-8; Grumman F11F the F-11, while A2F (second attack design by Grumman) was re-designated the A-6 Intruder.
4. Gunston, *American Warplanes*, pp.164-165.
5. Unless stated otherwise, this sub-chapter is based on Baker (1998); Bugos (1996); Buttler (2005); Gillcrist (1994); Gunston (*F-111*, 1983), Jenkins (1997); Peacock (1986); Richardson & Spick (1984); Spick (*F-14*, 1985); Spick, 'The Iron Tigers' (1991).
6. Buttler (2005); Gunston (*F-111*, 1983), Jenkins (1997); Peacock (1986); Spick (*F-14*, 1985).
7. Baker (1998); Gillcrist (1994); Gunston (*F-111*, 1983), Jenkins (1997); Peacock (1986); Spick (*F-14*, 1985).
8. Peacock (1986); Spick (*F-14*, 1985).
9. Spick (*F-14*, 1985).
10. Jenkins (1997); Peacock (1986); Spick (*F-14*, 1985).
11. Unless stated otherwise, this sub-chapter is based on Peacock (1986) & Spick (*F-14*, 1985).
12. Armistead (2002) & Francillon (1989).
13. Spick (*F-14*, 1985).
14. Spick (*F-14*, 1985), p.59; 'John F Kennedy I (CVA-67), 1968-2009', Naval History and Heritage Command, 1 October 2001; Calka, *F-100D/F* & Lièbert et all, *Super Mystère B2*
15. For details, see Gillcrist, *Tomcat!*.

CHAPTER 2

1. Unless stated otherwise, all data on Soviet-manufactured air-to-air missiles provided henceforth is based on Markovskiy et al, p.97.
2. Markovskiy et al, p.97; Mladenov, 'MiG-25 Foxbat', p.31.
3. Mladenov, 'MiG-25 Foxbat', p.31.
4. Fomin, 'MiG-29 Evolution' & MAPO, *MiG-29*.

CHAPTER 3

1. For a detailed military history of the Iran-Iraq War, see Hooton et al, *Iran-Iraq War*, Vols. 1-4.
2. Unless stated otherwise, all IRIAF-related details in this sub-chapter are based on Ghafouri, pp.294-296
3. Unless stated otherwise, based on AP, 'US Confirms Navy Jet fired at Iranian Fighter', Associated Press, 11 August 1987; 'Recollections of Pilot Major Darious Kaknegar' & Willcox, pp.202-204.
4. Willcox, pp.202-204. Apparently disappointed by the results of this clash, the IRIAF launched a major investigation into the circumstances. Later in 1987, an unknown officer serving at TFB.9 was arrested for clandestinely revealing flight information to the US intelligence. Full details about this affair have never been released and related files remain locked until today.

CHAPTER 4

1. For details on Iraqi-Kuwaiti relations and the Iraqi invasion of 2 August 1990, see Hooton et al, *Operation Desert Storm*, Vol. 1.
2. For details on the development and combat application of systems like APX-80 see Michel, *Clashes!*
3. Spick (*The Great Book of Modern Warplanes*), p.287; Hooton et al, *Desert Storm Vol.1*; Pokrant, p.6 & Parsons, interview, 11/2020.
4. Pokrant, pp.6-7.
5. According to Sammari (*Shattering the Eastern Gates*, p.250), the IrAF had 620 combat aircraft, 26 Ilyushin Il-76 and An-24 transports and 243 training aircraft. US intelligence reports usually put the figure at about 700, while Iraqi documentation captured in 2003 lists a total of 997, including 620 fighters (Woods, p.272).
6. ONI, Speartip 014-90.
7. Unless stated otherwise, all data based on Sadik, interview, 03/2006 & Sadik et al, 'The First Night'.
8. Sadik, interview, 03/2006 & 03/2007.
9. For a full operational history of MiG-23s in the Middle East (including Iraq), see Cooper, *MiG-23 in the Middle East*.
10. Markovskiy et al, p.97.
11. Sadik, interviews, 03/2006 & 03/2007.
12. ONI, Speartip 014-90 & Woods, pp.70, 89. For a full operational history of Mirage F.1 in Iraq, see Cooper et al, *Iraqi Mirages*.
13. Sadik, interviews, 03/2005, 03/2006 & 03/2007 & Sadik et al, 'The First Night'.
14. Sadik, interiews, 03/2006 & 03/2007.
15. Unless stated otherwise details on Kari are based on Sadik, interviews, 03/2005, 03/2006 & 03/2007; Ali Tobchi, multiple interviews since 2012; 'Iraq's Air Defence Command' in *Jane's Intelligence Review*, Vol.2, Part 2, pp.187-204-208, 210, 222-226.
16. Another 500 fire-control radars were supporting the work of SAM sites and anti-aircraft artillery batteries.
17. Raspletin; Hooton et al, *Desert Storm*, Vol.1.
18. Sadik, interviews, 03/2005, 03/2007 & 10/2007.
19. For full understanding of Sha'ban's and Basu's influence, and repercussions of Saddam's decision from early 1989, see Cooper et al, *Iraqi Mirages*.
20. Sadik, interviews, 03/2005, 03/2006 & 03/2007& Woods, pp.144-147, 167 f/n 81.
21. Sadik, interviews, 03/2005 & 03/2007.
22. Bary G Royden, *Tolkachev, A Worthy Successor to Penkovsky: An Exceptional Espionage Operation*, CIA Center for the Study of Intelligence, Studies in Intelligence Vol 47, No. 3, 14 April 2007.
23. Conclusions based on work on the *Iraqi Mirages* project (see Bibliography for details), cross-examination of interviews with Sadik and other former IrAF officers, and SPEARTIP 014-90.
24. Conclusions based on 'off the record' parts of interviews with a number of former Navy F-14-pilots and RIOs.
25. Ironically, before the Second Persian Gulf War of 1991, the Navy's fighter doctrine was – sometimes fiercely – opposed primarily by the Navy's fighter-bomber pilots. A-6 Intruder crews especially tended to challenge the Topgun staff, and the staff of F-14 units, and insisted on running their attacks without fighter escort. They suspected that the Tomcat's powerful AWG-9 would make the enemy aware of

an incoming air strike, thus resulting in the unwanted attention of the enemy air defences. As far as is known, all such opinions were quickly 'forgotten' as soon as A-6 crews had their first encounters with the Iraqi Foxbats: henceforth, some of them demanded F-14s 'to their right and left', no matter where they went.

26 Alwine, interview, 10/2018.

CHAPTER 5

1   Pokrant, pp.6, 23.
2   Alwine, interview, 11/2020.
3   Sadik, interviews, 03/2005 & 03/2006; Davis, pp.188-189; Pokrant, pp.13-14; Dildy et al, pp.48-49; Hamilton, interview with Ryan Gillcrist, 11/2018; Alwine, interview, 11/2020.
4   Alwine, interviews, 01/2020 & 11/2020. Notably, Alwine was the most junior pilot in VF-74, and thus crewed with a senior RIO: 'Traps' – a former test pilot and Topgun graduate – was regarded as one of the best F-14-RIOs in the Navy.
5   Sadik, interviews, 03/2005 & 03/2006 & Dildy et al, pp.49-50. Notably, according to Sadik, the Iraqis knew nothing about the shootdown of LCDR Speicher until interrogating the RIO of the downed F-14A+, on 21 January 1991. Even then, the Intelligence Directorate of the IrAF was astounded to find out that the Navy declared one of its pilots as shot down and killed in action over Iraq, because it had no reports of its own about the capture of such a pilot, or the finding of the wreckage and pilot's body. Correspondingly, Dawoud's claim was originally sorted under 'probable'. A thorough investigation was launched only in 1995, after the Intelligence Directorate learned about the downing of LCDR Speicher from the US media. Subsequently, Dawoud was credited with a confirmed kill, awarded, and decorated.
6   Ibid.
7   Pokrant, pp.15 & Alwine, interviews, 01/2020 & 11/2020.
8   Pokrant, p.17.
9   Off-record commentary by a USN F-14 pilot, name withheld.
10 Parsons, interview, 10/2018 & 11/2020.
11 Fitzpatrick, interview with Ryan Gillcrist, 06/2019; Hamilton, interview with Ryan Gillcrist, 08/2019.
12 Ibid.
13 Mongillo flew the F/A-18C AA410, McKee 163470/AA400, and Fox the 163508/AA401.
14 Sadik, interview, 10/2007 & Brown, pp.36-38.
15 Wyatt, interview, 04/2020.
16 Pokrant, pp.18-19 & Glaser, interviews, 11/2019 & 01/2020.
17 Sadik, interview, 10/2007.
18 Pokrant, pp.19-20, 22.
19 Glaser, interviews, 11/2019 & 01/2020.
20 Air base 'names' like H-1, H-2, H-3 and similar might sound unusual, but it should be kept in mind that these designations were never used in official Iraqi documentation. All three locations were named after oil pipelines constructed by the British in the 1930s: their starting point was Kirkuk, in north-eastern Iraq, and thus the first branch of this pipeline was designated K, and the pumping stations supporting it K-1, K-2, K-3 etc. This pipeline ended at Haditha, in north-western Iraq, where it branched into two other pipelines: the T-pipeline for Tripoli in Lebanon, and the H-pipeline for Haifa in the Palestine. Correspondingly, the pumping stations on these two pipelines were designated T-1, T-2, T-3 etc, and H-1, H-2, H-3 etc., respectively. Each of the pumping stations originally had a small landing strip used for aircraft that transported technicians and maintenance equipment, or provided logistical support. While most of the H and K pipelines had not operated since the Arab-Israeli Wars of 1948 and 1967, their airfields were subsequently taken over by the local armed forces and gradually expanded into major air bases.
21 Sadik, interview, 03/2007.
22 Davis, pp.210-215 & Sadik, interviews, 03/2005, 03/2006 & 03/2007.
23 Dildy et al, pp.51-53.
24 Dildy et al, pp.51-53.
25 Sadik, interview, 03/2007.
26 The SPN-30 served the purpose of jamming airborne radars and worked exactly like a missile-guidance system: it relied on its antenna being directed at the incoming aircraft.
27 Sadik, interview, 03/2007.
28 *Gulf Air War Debrief*, pp.96-97 & Sadik, interview, 03/2007, quoting from IrAF, *Methods and Tactics employed by Enemy Air Forces* (see Documents for details).
29 Sadik, interview, 03/2007. Notably, the Soviets recommended their export customers not to turn off the emitter once this was jammed by enemy ECM, in order not to reveal to the enemy that the jamming was effective. Instead, they recommended the use of a special mode, which ceased emissions from the radar. However, it remains unclear if the Iraqis received P-12s with such working modes.
30 Sadik, interview, 03/2007.
31 *Gulf Air War Debrief*, pp.96-99.
32 Rick Morgan (former EA-6B pilot and historian), interview, 04/2020.
33 Sadik, interview, 03/2007.
34 Alwine, interviews, 04/2020 & 11/2020.
35 Sadik, interview, 03/2007, quoting from IrAF, *Methods and Tactics employed by Enemy Air Forces* (see Documents for details); Morgan, interview, 04/2020 & Ali Tobchi, interview, 11/2019. Notably, with Dawoud's claim from the morning of 17 January being classed as 'probable', and with Ibrahim returning with all his R-40s still on their launch rails, the IrAF became convinced that its Foxbats had not scored even a single kill by that point in time. Unsurprisingly, this was what many of its MiG-25 pilots – including Major Mohammed Sid Ahmed – who served with No. 96 Squadron as of 1991, and was interviewed by Sadik on behalf of the author in 2006 – were reporting even a decade later. Furthermore, Sadik was one of the IrAF officers interrogating captured Coalition airmen, including LT Devon Jones. According to Sadik, Jones told him his Tomcat was weighed down by a TARPS pod, and thus sluggish when manoeuvring at slow speeds – such as when escorting a Prowler. Furthermore, Jones told him that he made a mistake due to fatigue: instead of continuing his left-hand orbit, he turned right. To the Iraqi, this was a 'perfectly plausible explanation': indeed, one that explained why the Tomcat entered the range of Saleh's SA-2 SAM site. Apparently, this is what contributed to the IrAF eventually crediting Major Saleh and the 62nd Missile Battery with the kill.
36 Based on CAPT Dale 'Snort' Snodgrass, 'My most tense Moment in the 26 Years of flying F-14s', SimHQ,com, 08/2000.

CHAPTER 6

1   Broce, interview, 07/2019
2   Unless stated otherwise, all IrAF-related details in this sub-chapter are based on Sadik, interview, 03/2005.
3   Pokrant, pp.49-50 & Martins, interview, 11/2020.
4   *Gulf Air War Debrief*, pp.236 & Sadik, interview, 10/2007.
5   *VF-1 Cruise Book*, entry for 7 February 1991.

CHAPTER 7

1 Holmes, pp.57-60.
2 Sadik, interview, 03/2007 & Ali Tobchi, interview, 11/2020.
3 'Factsheets: Operation Desert Fox', afhso.af.mil, 15 August 2013.
4 Unless stated otherwise, this sub-chapter is based on Neil 'Waylon' Jennings' unfinished manuscript *Slipping the Bonds*, found by Ryan Gilchrist in cooperation with Suzanne Jennings; Mike Bilzor (USN historian), Jonathan Shoemaker, Tim Aslin, Vincent Aiello, Jonathan Ross, Nicholas Mongillo, and Robert Soderholm, interviews, 09-11/2019; Ali Tobchi, interview, 10/2019
5 The reason why the Hornet was flying with the Tomcat was that the wingman's F-14D went down before the launch.
6 Loessberg, interviews, 01/2020 and 11/2020.

ABOUT THE AUTHOR

Tom Cooper is an Austrian aerial warfare analyst and historian. Following a career in the worldwide transportation business – during which he established a network of contacts in the Middle East and Africa – he moved into narrow-focus analysis and writing on small, little-known air forces and conflicts, about which he has collected extensive archives. This has resulted in specialisation in such Middle Eastern air forces as of those of Egypt, Iran, Iraq, and Syria, plus various African and Asian air forces.

In addition to authoring and co-authoring about 50 books – including about three dozen titles for Helion's @War series – and well over 1,000 articles. Cooper has been the editor of the five @War series since 2017, and this is his 35th book for Helion.